the Other Woman in your Marriage

the Other Woman in your Marriage

Understanding a Mother's Impact On Her Son & How It Affects His Marriage

H. Norman Wright

Author of the #1 Best-sellers *Always Daddy's Girl* and *Quiet Times for Couples*

Regal Books
A Division of Gospel Light
Ventura, California, U.S.A.

Published by Regal Books
A Division of Gospel Light
Ventura, California, U.S.A.
Printed in U.S.A.

Regal Books is a ministry of Gospel Light, an evangelical Christian publisher dedicated to serving the local church. We believe God's vision for Gospel Light is to provide church leaders with biblical, user-friendly materials that will help them evangelize, disciple and minister to children, youth and families.

It is our prayer that this Regal Book will help you discover biblical truth for your own life and help you meet the needs of others. May God richly bless you.

For a free catalog of resources from Regal Books/Gospel Light please contact your Christian supplier or call 1-800-4-GOSPEL.

Library of Congress Cataloging-in-Publication Data
Wright, H. Norman.
    The other woman in your marriage / H. Norman Wright.
        p. cm.
    Includes bibliographical references.
    ISBN 0-8307-1494-4 (Hard Cover)
    1. Mothers and sons. 2. Parent and adult child. 3. Mothers-in-law.
4. Daughters-in-law. 5. Parenting—Religious aspects—Christianity. I. Title.
HQ755.85W78 1994
306.874'3—dc20   93-44832
                                                                                  CIP

1 2 3 4 5 6 7 8 9 10 11 12 13 14 / 02 01 00 99 98 97 96 95 94

Rights for publishing this book in other languages are contracted by Gospel Literature International (GLINT). GLINT also provides technical help for the adaptation, translation and publishing of Bible study resources and books in scores of languages worldwide. For further information, contact GLINT, P.O. Box 4060, Ontario, CA 91761-1003, U.S.A., or the publisher.

Contents

Part I Understanding Your Husband

Chapter 1 *Mothers, Sons and Daughters-in-Law*　　　9
"Deep down, men's feelings and expectations about themselves and the women in their lives can often be attributed to their childhood experiences with their mother."

Chapter 2 *Memories of Mom*　　　37
"The best step a mother can take is to validate her son's quest for independence and encourage the separation process."

Chapter 3 *The Father/Son Relationship*　　　65
"A young son needs his father's respect for his feelings, rather than hearing the age-old myth, 'Big boys don't cry.'"

Part II Understanding Your In-Laws

Chapter 4 *Establishing Freedom in Marriage*　　　93
"Marriage partners should usually do what increases happiness between them, even if it disturbs their parents' happiness."

Chapter 5 *Guidelines for Adult Married Children*   **113**
"Three ingredients are necessary for any relationship to grow: time, attention and implementing biblical principles in the relationship."

Chapter 6 *Making Peace with Your Mother-in-Law*   **133**
"We have all inherited relationships either by bloodlines or through marriage in which we truly wish we had been left out of the will."

Part III   Understanding Your Own Son

Chapter 7 *Sons: To Have, to Hold and to Let Go*   **159**
"Part of the difficulty with our parental expectations is that they come out of the emptiness of our own need... rather than seeking the face of God and His will for who and what a son is to become."

Chapter 8 *When Your Sons Are Grown*   **183**
"Keep in mind that your value and worth is not based upon your son's perception, or on how well you did as a parent."

Chapter 9 *"I Never Expected This!"*   **205**
"The goal of parents whose son's lifestyle they reject should be to make their value system clear, and to show loving concern, without being lured into the codependency trap."

Epilogue *A Tribute to My Own Mother*   **231**

Discussion Leader's Guide   **237**

Part I

Understanding Your Husband

chapter

1

Mothers, Sons and Daughters-in-law

THE SOUND FROM THE TELEVISION IS DEAFENING AS SHOUTS AND SCREAMS ERUPT from 80,000 people. Many are jumping up and down. A spirit of mayhem rules on the playing field. An electrifying play has just vaulted the home team to an overwhelming lead. One of the defensive backs intercepted a pass, cut through an army of opposing players and sprinted across the goal line.

That was the easy part. Now he is fighting his way back to the sideline through an exuberant crowd of players and coaches that are hopelessly out of control.

Finally, the hero of the moment makes it to the bench and takes off his helmet, rivets of sweat pouring down his face. He grabs an oxygen tank, takes a few whiffs to get his wind back and grins broadly to acknowledge the congratulations of the other players.

Suddenly, he senses that the TV camera is focusing on him. He turns his six-foot five-inch muscular frame toward the camera, smiles, waves and says, "Hi, Mom!" Soon his friends stick their heads in the camera and echo his words: "Hi, Mom! Hi, Mom!"

On the battlefields and hospitals of the Civil War, World Wars I and II, Korea and Vietnam, wounded and dying soldiers cry out the same word in their own native tongue: "Mother!" "¡Madre!" "Mom!" "Mama!"

Why is it that in times of both ecstasy and agony in a man's life he so often calls out either a greeting or a plea to his mother? Why not call more often to his wife, or father? Mother seems to still be connected to him in some way. Perhaps it's because she was the first one to love and comfort him when he entered into this life, and was his primary source of nurture during his early years.

Mother Power

Mothers have such a powerful influence upon their sons that it often continues to shape—for good or ill—their decisions, work and family relationships throughout adulthood.

We think of Winston Churchill as a great leader who helped shape the course of world history. It is less often noted that he was in turn shaped to a great extent by his mother, Jennie Jerome—a noted and beautiful daughter of a powerful New York financier

As a child, young Winston was both brilliant and obnoxious. He lived in a home with a distant, rejecting father (which perhaps contributed to Winston's overbearing behavioral problem). But his mother never gave up on him. It was she who introduced him to politicians and prime ministers. She discussed politics with him. During his career she continued to send him books that shaped his style of writing and speech. Over the years, she used her contacts and influence to get him transferred from one war to another. She helped in his placement as a war correspondent, and actively served as his agent for his early writings.

Churchill's mother worked alongside him in his early political campaigns. Some would say her influence was entirely too dominant as she not only encouraged him and shared her own stamina with him, but actually pushed him.[1] He gave credit to his mother and uttered a sad commentary on his relationship with his father when he said, "I owe everything to my mother and nothing to my father."[2]

Throughout the history of our own country we see examples of the close relationship of sons and mothers. Some of this deeply rooted connectedness was admirable, and some was dysfunctional.

A boy learns feelings almost exclusively from his mother. From her, he gains a sense of nurture and protection that is actually experienced as care for the soul.

Former President General Dwight Eisenhower took time out from the planning of the allied invasion of France in May of 1944 to send his mother a Mother's Day greeting. Industrialist Andrew Carnegie's mother begged him not to marry until after her death—which he did. One year after her death he finally married...at the age of 52.

Another president, Franklin Delano Roosevelt, made very few decisions unless he discussed them first with his mother. When he fell in love with the woman who became his wife, he was almost paranoid about his mother discovering it, so he wrote about Eleanor in code in his journal.[3]

A mother tends to look after her son's best interests, no matter how old he is. Not all attempts are actually beneficial, but the intent is clear. In his autobiography, former Los Angeles Police Chief Darrell Gates tells what happened following his divorce. He wasn't really interested in dating, and spent most of his time by himself. Women were attracted to him but he was very involved in his work. Gates' mother began to worry about him, as most mothers do. Her "solution" to his dating so rarely was to buy him a subscription to *Playboy* magazine.[4]

Robert Bly graphically describes what a son learns from his mother:

> When the world of men is submerged in the world of technology and business, it seems to the boy that cool excitement lies there, and warm excitement with the mother; money with the father, food with the mother; anxiety with the father, assurance with the mother; conditional love with the father, and unconditional love with the mother.[5]

Bly goes on to say that a boy learns *feelings* almost exclusively from his mother. From her, he gains a sense of nurture and protection that is actually experienced as *care for the soul.*

Bly's research indicates that in our society, as a rule, the boy receives these qualities, if he receives them at all, from the mother. His emotional bonding is therefore with her, not with the father.

When a Mother Dies

The significance of a son's mother is often apparent when the mother dies. For the son, it is the loss of the person who shaped his early years and taught him his earliest tasks such as how to talk, walk and behave. His mother may have been his dominant guide, main refuge—or primary critic. In many homes a mother, more than the father, fulfills the role of the communicator or intermediary or the confidante. Some sons feel set adrift when a mother dies or leaves, because they never developed a meaningful conversational relationship with a father. Now he is all they have left. And the younger the son when a mother dies, the more difficult it is.

A dramatic, if negative, example of the effect of a mother's death was exemplified in the life of Houdini, the great magician. He had an extraordinary attachment for his mother that affected his entire life. And after she died, he seemed to cover his grief with extreme risk-taking behavior.

Of course, this kind of behavior began much earlier. Houdini spent much of his life escaping from all varieties of restraints, including straitjackets, chains, handcuffs, manacles, chests, glass boxes, roll-top desks and iron lockers. He jumped from bridges having his arms thoroughly secured. He allowed himself to be suspended having his head down, then freed himself from meshes of restraining apparatus. He was chained and buried six feet deep in the earth, locked in steel vaults, as well as nailed in huge packing cases. It seemed that no risk was too great, too bizarre or too difficult. After the death of his mother, this behavior seemed to be a thinly disguised drive for self-destruction.[6] The world is full of countless numbers of men who feel the same way.

Living Reflections

As a wife, what image of your mother-in-law do you see reflected in your husband? Remember, you aren't called to criticize her. Neither is it your task to "fix" any traits your husband may have inherited from her, or to upbraid him for the way he has been shaped by his mother. But reflecting on her influence on him may help you understand and relate better to him. And it may help you, as a woman who may one day be a mother-in-law yourself, to be aware of both the negative and the positive possibilities of influencing your son, and relating to a daughter-in-law.

Obviously, as Bly reminded us, a mother has so much to offer a son. Too often, however, she is not given the guidance she needs.

Your mother-in-law may have had only her instincts to guide her in seeing that her influence is a positive instead of a negative force in her son's life.

It is also helpful for a husband to ask himself about the ways his mother helped shape his personality. It can be a liberating experience to ask about the level of attachment between the two.

This is the journey you're about to embark upon: looking at the significance of the mother-son relationship, and how she shapes the direction of his life.

Stages of a Relationship

From the moment of birth, a child sets out to accomplish his first task of life: to develop a mutually beneficial relationship with his mother. This kind of relationship is called "symbiotic," literally "life together."

The initial three to four months of a child's life is spent sleeping more than being awake. Although his awareness of what is going on is very limited, the beginnings of a relationship are being forged. Even at this young age the infant has an inborn drive that causes him to seek the alleviation of discomfort. And mother is usually the one to provide the comfort.

But the child isn't the only one who has this need for attachment. The mother has the same desire. She changes her schedule, her way of talking—her entire lifestyle—to meet her child's needs. This stage is vital for both mother and child.

Traditionally, the father's role has been primarily as a backup to Mom. He is sometimes referred to as the "second mom." In fact, an infant doesn't really differentiate between his mother and father until around the fourth or fifth month.

Then the father's role becomes one of protecting and encouraging this important mother-son connection. Fortunately, in modern times we are seeing greater involvement from fathers right from the birth of the child. This creates a greater sense of bonding; but even with Dad's increased involvement, the child normally continues to show a preference for his mother.

Venturing Out

At six to eight months, this totally dependent child (whom we'll call Jimmy) begins to venture out to accomplish the next task: establishing himself as a separate person. Now you see the beginning of independence emerging, and it's rooted in the security of his relationship with his mother. Jimmy dares to venture out and expand horizons largely because his mother has made him feel safe. He is now becoming an explorer and a pioneer searching out new experiences.

Rarely, however, does he venture very far away. He can't let Mother out of his sight for very long. He will go away and then come back to make sure Mother is still there. He'll go away again but look around to make sure his source of comfort and security is still there. Even Mother's voice gives reassurance.

At this early age, Jimmy is aware that Mother isn't always kind, loving and nurturing. He is totally dependent upon her, and doesn't see himself as separate from her. That's how close they are. This is why he has to keep going back again and again to check up on her.

From a child's perspective, the first few months of life are marked by Mom's doing a series of disappearing acts. Although he is learning a new sense of freedom, it can be stressful if Mother is gone too long or can't be found. And although he can't put his experience into words, that uneasy sense of fear of abandonment we all face has made its presence known.

Echoes from the Past

Events that occur during this stage can have a lasting effect, although at the moment there may not be a conscious recognition of what is actually happening. Even hearing about it a few years later may be devastating. The adopted son of former President Ronald Reagan told about his struggle and journey toward self-acceptance. He said, "I grew up convinced that my birth mother gave me away because she didn't love me and I was bad."[7]

The intensity and pain of his plight are further illustrated in a recurring nightmare in which Michael Reagan's family is about to enter heaven—all except him:

> The gates open, and I step aside to let my family precede me. Suddenly God steps in front of me, placing His burning hand on my chest. My son Cameron turns around. "Come on, Dad," he says impatiently and starts toward me. But God is still halting my progress. He turns his back to me and takes out my Book of Life from deep within his white robes. He opens the book and shows my family a page. His voice booms in my ears. "Michael Reagan is not allowed into heaven because he is illegitimate."[8]

Fortunately, Michael goes on to say that he did discover that he was loved and wanted. But it took 40 years before he could have peace about his early childhood.

To Be Like Dad

By about 18 months, a child has a need to begin moving away from his mother. A little boy begins to realize that he is a bit different from his mother and in some unique way he is drawn to his father. Here are the beginnings of wanting to be like his father. But if a significant vacant spot exists where father is supposed to be, many serious problems can occur later on. These include homosexuality, adolescent drug abuse, poor academic performance and childhood depression.[9]

Boys raised by women learn to adapt their behavior to accommodate women. Unfortunately, they usually tend to suppress some normal male behavior that bothers women. As a result, they sometimes become men who know how to please women, but not themselves. They may also have difficulty relating to other men and often lack close male friendships.[10] As much as a mother might try to fill this gap, it's too much to ask of her.

Robin Skynner, a psychologist, describes the process of gender identification in terms of a mother and her children standing on one bank of a river, the father standing on the opposite bank. The mother and her daughters stay on the same bank when appropriate identification occurs, but a boy must ford the river in order to identify with his father. This break is so dramatic that the boy may feel he must shun anything that smacks of femaleness. Obviously, this process can become an emotional ordeal for all concerned.[11]

Many mothers can identify with what Judith Balswick adds to this description:

> The mother, in anticipation of this separation, may guard against becoming overly connected with her son in order to protect herself from the pain of letting him go. If she holds on too tightly, he may have difficulty perceiving himself as a male. Friends may call this child "a mama's boy" unless he musters the courage to make this emotional break and identify with his father or some other male role model. Chodorow has noted that this may be one reason males tend to resist being dependent on women.[12]

Enter the Father

As Jimmy approaches his second year of life, he needs to move farther and farther away from his mother so his sense of individuality can develop. But because he is so young and still dependent, he needs to have someone else to cling to for his emotional security. This is where Father comes in. Instead of hanging on tightly to Mother, young Jimmy eases his grip so just the fingertips of one hand are touching hers. The fingertips of his other hand are now touching his father's. This is a normal process, and the way it's supposed to work.

But what if Jimmy's father isn't available because he's emotionally distant, doesn't care, works too much, is divorced or deceased? Jimmy may remain too involved and attached to his mother. The emotional fusion could continue too long and be too intense with his mother. Mother may become too involved and powerful, and Jimmy may become too dependent upon her. His

> *Fathers need to play a vital role in how children formulate their sexual identity. A father will affect how Jimmy will grow up to see himself as a man.*

development may become stunted at this point because he is unable to develop his independence.

Now the emotion of fear begins to take up residence in and control Jimmy's life. If he were able to think it through and express it, his thoughts might be something like this: "Boy, what if I do something to really upset Mom. Maybe *she* wouldn't want to be around me, either. I couldn't handle that. I've always got to please her."[13]

Transition and Helping Hands

In an earlier time, a father's role was simply that of a buffer between an infant or child and his mother. When Jimmy got frustrated and angry with his mother, he was able to go to his father, drain off his anger and then feel comfortable in going back to his mother. But if there was no father, those angry feelings would either come out against mother, or Jimmy might learn to bottle them up and turn them back against himself.

Here is a warning for single mothers: be prepared to encourage

Jimmy to find positive ways to ventilate such feelings. Some churches have "mentor" or "buddy" programs in which men can provide in a surrogate way some of what boys without fathers need to help them bond with older males.

Ideally, of course, a father is more than just a buffer. Fathers need to play a vital role in how children formulate their sexual identity. A father will affect how Jimmy will grow up to see himself as a man. A boy longs to bond with a man. He needs to grow and see himself as a man among other men, for this gives him a sense of identity.

The transition from identifying with the mother to the father is not a conscious decision. God's plan for a son is to desire to identify with his father. Between the ages of five and eight, this God-created desire for identification shifts from the mother to the father.

Around the age of nine, a son begins to question and challenge his mother's authority. This is a time when a son wants his father's approval rather than his mother's. This is perfectly normal.

A son needs a helping hand from his father or some other male figure to make this transition. He feels comfort with his mother, but Jimmy senses that in some way identifying with his father is a comfort, too. This is part of normal and healthy development. Jimmy needs to move from his mother to his father as the primary influence in his life.

But separation does not mean severance. It should be done in a gradual, gentle and natural way, both mother and father helping in the process. A son is like a sponge: he absorbs from his father what it's like to be a man. And he will tend to follow the pattern set by his father, whether it's healthy or unhealthy.

A son needs to be drawn into the role and responsibilities of the male world with sensitivity, compassion, firmness, acceptance and father-love. For many young sons, moving away from Mother is scary. Father's world is both enticing and frightening at the same time. In this new world a boy learns more about the male body as well as the man's way of thinking and responding to life. He learns how the male mind functions.[14]

When the Father Is Absent

If he has no father or other positive male role model, Jimmy may turn elsewhere in his quest to identify with other males. We see this in the increase of gangs. Destructive though it is, this grouping provides roots, identity and a relationship with other males.

We see this especially in African-American families. Some 55 percent of Black families today are headed by women. Prentice Tipton, a Black minister, describes the problem in this way:

> When mothers lead the family because the fathers fail to lead—either by absenting themselves from the home or by taking a passive role—boys are deprived of the most important natural model of manliness. Growing up mainly under the supervision of women, many of them experience insecurity over their identity as men.[15]

Rev. Tipton goes on to say that one tendency for boys growing up without the presence of a father is to rebel against the women who are their authorities. A boy may become socially disruptive and irresponsible in the home, at school, or at work. They may be driven to "prove" their manhood, especially in areas of sexuality. It is all too easy to become caught up in violence, crime, alcoholism and other addictions.

An opposite tendency, Rev. Tipton warns, is for young men to identify with the adult women who are the authorities in their lives, instinctively behaving and reacting in ways that are more appropriate to women than to men. He concludes:

> To the extent that young males take either option, they do not learn the discipline, the responsibility, and the character involved in being a man. They are left groping for manhood in a variety of socially disruptive ways.[16]

If a mother is single, she needs a father substitute for her sons. Bobbie Reed, who experienced a divorce, shares:

> Because the boys' father lived too far away for frequent
> visits during the early years after our divorce, I knew
> (they) needed additional men in their lives. I hired male
> sitters, signed them up for Little League, swimming and
> diving teams with male coaches, and found a man in the
> church with sons who would include one or both of my
> boys in some of their "men only" activities such as camp-
> ing, fishing, and hiking.[17]

Of course, difficulties can occur between a mother and a son
whether the father is absent or not. But when the father isn't there
physically or emotionally it leaves the son yearning for a model of
what it means to be a man. Frequently, a son will then enter into
some unspoken and secret agreement with his mother to fulfill those
unsatisfied needs.

The Blame Game

Some mothers are actually blamed when such an unspoken arrangement fails; they simply are not men, and they can't meet all of a son's
expectations. I have talked with adult men who appear to be angry
with their mother for what she supposedly failed to give them. In
time, however, the real source of anger emerges. It is really against
their father for abandoning them. Their mothers end up taking all
the blame, which of course is not justified.

Look at the pattern of mother blaming. Researchers from the
Ontario Institute for Studies in Education reviewed 125 articles in
journals of clinical psychology from the years 1970, 1976 and 1982.
Regardless of the journal, the year or who wrote the article, mother
blaming was the focus. It was amazing to discover that 72 types of dis-
orders were laid directly at the feet of the mothers. Mothers were
related to a child's problems five times as often as fathers.[18]

Consider the ways a mother is blamed:

> Psychologists traditionally blame the mother when her

children have problems. Sociologists blame her for the breakdown of the family when she works outside the home. Feminists blame her for keeping her children dependent when she chooses to work in the home, raising her children. Husbands blame her for depriving them by putting the children first. Children blame her for making mistakes and not giving them enough of what they need or want. When it so often seems like she's being set up as the designated scapegoat, it's a wonder any woman dares take on the task of motherhood.[19]

A 41-year-old man, speaking about the difficulties he experienced with his mother and father, told me recently, "A mother assists her son in creating a vision for his life. A father helps his son execute it. But if what they are to give is not in harmony with one another a son ends up confused and frustrated. If the father is absent or unavailable, the son is incomplete. That's the way I feel."

"It's a Boy!"

A boy's relationship with his mother may be shaped in part by whether his parents wanted a son or a daughter when he was born. Surveys indicate that 80 percent of those in our country want their firstborn to be a boy. Perhaps it has to do with the significance of the firstborn.

In some cultures this preference is even more marked. And in our country we would probably expect this from the male population. But consider that 90 percent of *women* preferred to have a boy first. In the book *Mothers and Sons*, the authors write, "A son is the clay with which many women fashion their most intricate life designs."[20]

Many women have been both delighted and relieved when their first child is a boy. Some have said their feelings of self-worth were intensified by their firstborn's being a son. One woman told me, "My husband would have been so disappointed if our child had been a girl. Who would carry on the family name?" Such words have been echoed by many.

Check the baby cards at a greeting-card shop. How do they describe a baby boy? Usually using words such as, "pride and joy," whereas the cards for girls have words such as, "small and sweet."

When people talk about a miscarriage it is common to hear statements such as, "The miscarriage was such a tragic event. It would have been a boy."

We still run into the problem of parents treating their sons differently from their daughters. Boys tend to experience fewer demands to care for other people, and usually have fewer limits set on their behavior.[21]

One woman who was interviewed about her relationship with her son admitted, "It is as if, through him, I've found the missing half of myself." Perhaps this feeling accounts for some of the overly close relationships we see between some mothers and sons. Sometimes it appears that the mother is trying to influence, through her son, the male dominated world in which she lives.[22]

Ken Druck suggests:

> Born into the male mystique, many men are commissioned from an early age to go out on a secret mission for Mother. This mission may be something as simple as succeeding in a profession Mother would have pursued had she been a man. Or it may be as complex as trying to shape themselves into the kind of man Mother REALLY wanted to marry. Often men do not know what drives them to please and impress women, or to rebel against them. In reality, it is because they often are unknowingly carrying out Mother's "secret assignment."
>
> Our mothers had a vital influence on how we perceive ourselves as men and the male roles we went on to assume as adults in our own families.[23]

Male-Female Tensions

Some issues between mothers and sons seem to stem from personal and cultural issues that exist between the sexes. Understanding some of these issues can help smooth relationships between a wife and her husband, who may still bear some of the effects of this tension.

"Correcting" Maleness

Today we seem to run into many women who are attempting to change through their son what angers them about men and male tendencies. They want their son to grow up and be "different" from other men—more sensitive, perhaps, and more tuned, to feminine ways. Such moms may overexpose their son to feminine activities, toys such as dolls, and other influences in an attempt to bring balance into their son's life.

Although certainly nothing is wrong with boys playing with dolls, the damage occurs when such mothers *limit* their sons at the same time from participating in activities and playing with toys traditionally associated with men. Not only does this approach not work, but it can also stunt the development of the boy and create many conflicts.

Many today are concerned about establishing and maintaining equality between men and women. Unfortunately, enforced equality often overlooks unchangeable gender differences.

On the other hand, some areas can be modified so that it is easier for men and women to relate and communicate. Over the years, I've seen how married couples can find a fulfilling relationship because they identified the other person's communication pattern and style, and learned to use it when they spoke with their spouse. This usually involved the husband learning a number of "feeling" words, and learning to create word pictures. (For additional assistance in learning this skill see chapter 8 of *Holding on to Romance* by this author.[24])

Mothers can help a son in this area when he is young by encouraging him in his language and vocabulary development. If a mother would encourage the father to develop this skill and model it for his son also, the boy would not only be able to relate better to women in general, but he would also be better equipped for school and for his life's work.

Getting Back at Dad

When Mom has experienced disappointment in a husband or father, it is all too easy for her to begin using her son as the means to fulfill her disappointment and emptiness. Speaking for men, Ken Druck writes:

> We hold Dad hostage to Mother's bitterness. We see him through her eyes. And this can provide a dangerous distortion, especially if there has been a divorce. We can easily end up with what the poet Robert Bly has called "a wounded image of our father," caused less by his actions than by our mother's perception of those actions.[25]

Druck goes on to warn of hidden resentments mothers may take out on their sons: "Your father spends too much time in the office." "Your father doesn't really love me." Druck tells of Randy, a 37-year-old high school science teacher, who discovered that most of his dissatisfaction with his father was actually his mother's dissatisfaction:

> "My parents were divorced when I was seven. My mother was always telling me what a selfish and dishonest man my father was. That went on for years. Whenever I was with my father, I found myself looking for dishonest things he might do, almost like I was trying to catch him at something bad."[26]

Carrying Mom into Life

Most men never really share significant information about their deepest feelings about their mother. Deep down, however, their feelings and expectations about themselves and the women in their lives can often be attributed to their childhood experiences with their mother. How a son perceives his mother affects his future.

Functional and Dysfunctional Memories

Some sons come from families where Mother reflected traditional family values. She ran the home and carried out the role of cook, chauffeur, coach, laundress and director of the children's lives. She loved being a mother and was thankful she could be at home.

Such moms were bent on making home a haven for the children and her husband. She would let it be known when she was displeased, and wouldn't avoid differences of opinion. She didn't dump her problems or any marital conflicts on the children. Sometimes she sacrificed the fulfillment of her own needs for other family members, but didn't complain about it or use it against them. She gained satisfaction from the children's accomplishments and they felt secure in her love.

If a son has a mother such as this, he usually is able to separate from her, as well as to relate to her in a positive way. He feels good about women in general. He likes and trusts them.

But if a son has a mother who did all the above but made her husband and children pay the price by being a martyr, then what? Some mothers constantly remind others of all she does for them in a play for sympathy. She creates guilt and the feeling, "You owe me." This is her way of controlling others in order to meet her needs. Other family members are made to feel they are responsible for her unhappiness.

What does this do to the son? He ends up carrying a load of guilt. Throughout his life he feels indebted to Mother, while at the same time knowing that nothing he does will ever please her. This colors his attitude and response toward all women. The anger, resentment and caution he has toward them is not surprising.

Neither should it surprise us when a man who has this kind of background has difficulty fully committing himself to a marriage relationship. He may fear that such commitment would require him to take on more guilt and even to give up his identity, just as he felt he had to do in relating to his mother.

The Overprotective Mom

Some mothers tend to take their role as nurturer and protector to an extreme. Mom may hover over her son because she is sure something bad will happen to him unless she protects him. Sports are out because he might get hurt. When he is an adult, she still watches over him. She tries to keep him tied to her, conveying the subtle but firm message, "Don't grow up."

How might this affect the son when he becomes a man? Too often he ends up believing, "I can't make it by myself." He may lack self-confidence, and consciously or subconsciously feel he needs his mother present in order to function. Often men come for counseling because of their helpless, dependent relationships with the women in their lives. I have seen mature, gifted men who function very ineffectively discover as we talk that they are still functioning as though Mother were still there. In some ways, she was!

At War with Mom?

In every generation we have adult men who are literally at war with their mothers. Druck describes it like this:

> Daily, we battle Mother's presence in our minds, fighting off the criticism we still hear ringing in our ears, her overprotectiveness that taught us to mistrust our instincts, and the burden of guilt she tried to lay upon our shoulders.

"Love-hate relationships" are often born out of silent

wars. Men who secretly are at war with their mothers feel
love on the one hand and hatred on the other. One side
yearns for Mother, fantasizing an ideal mother-son relationship. The other side is repulsed by her, seeking
vengeance on the woman he blames for everything that
went awry in his life. The battle rages on secretly inside
him.

Men who become fantasy soldiers in an imaginary war
against their own mothers are unwilling to risk the little
security they feel they have. But they need some way to
do battle with what they perceive as their mother's
destructive behavior toward them. Secret wars are their
chosen defense against the women who would threaten
them.[27]

Wives easily can suffer the fallout from such warfare. When a
son's relationship with his mother was not healthy or was lacking in
some way, the women in his life should beware! A boy who is too
close to his mother or who has no father may turn back to his mother in early adulthood, because he has no father with whom to connect. But if he looks to his mother for his masculinity, he will experience confusion. And if he is confused he may look to his wife for
support and strength, which may then feed a feeling of inadequacy.

When a man expects his wife to pick up where his mother left
off, a wife could be punished for his mother's deficiencies or offens-
es. All a wife has to do is respond in some way that reminds her husband of his mother, and she takes the heat.

Some husbands treat their wives in ways they wish they could
have treated their mother, but never did. They become angry, explo-
sive, defensive, verbally abusive and pushy. One author describes
these responses as "ghost feelings" that linger on because of the mother-son relationship.

Mother's ghost can take a thousand and one forms. The
man who turns his wife into a permission giver has yet

to exorcise his mother's ghost from his marriage. Men with controlling mothers may secretly promise themselves never again to give that much power to any woman.[28]

One of the most frustrating responses for the wife is when her husband is helpless and dependent. He is a taker. He wants to be taken care of as he may have been at home. He has never learned to give and connect with a woman in a healthy way.

A son is not a mother's possession. He is not an extension of herself, nor is he to be the fulfillment of her unfulfilled life.

If an adult man is living with the ghost of his mother, it's time for him to assume responsibility for his own adult life. In blunt terms, it is time for him to grow up. Mothers are not perfect, and they bring their own baggage into motherhood. Furthermore, their problems can be intensified by an absent or uninvolved husband. Blame won't solve the problem but identifying, recognizing and taking action will.

A Mother's Role

Perhaps this can all be summed up in the answer to the question: What is the role of a mother in raising a son?

First, she is called by Scripture to nurture, train, love, comfort, correct and teach her child. In Proverbs 31, the Bible describes what King Lemuel learned from his mother. He learned from her how to rule and marry. She helped him learn to evaluate options open to him as a king. She let him know that not all the women interested in him would be good for him, and that he needed to look for one who was capable, and who had his best interest in mind. She planted in his heart a concern for those who were poor, dumb, embittered and wretched. This kind of wisdom from mothers has been a guide to many in positions of authority and influence.

Most mothers are in the key position of having the opportunity to provide the child with his first living example of who persons are, and who they can become.

But a son is not a mother's possession. He is not an extension of herself, nor is he to be the fulfillment of her unfulfilled life. These attitudes can make a son into a "little idol" in one form or another, Mom living for what her son becomes, and basking in his accomplishment. Such mothers have too much invested in their sons.

Perhaps the crucial question is, To whom does a son belong? For all believers, the answer is God. Our children are a gift from God. They are only lent to us. The task for parents is to love them, nurture them, raise them—and then, just like the space shuttle, to launch them. Let them become all that God wants them to become.[29]

Although a mother is usually the first person to connect with her son, in a way she is similar to a member of a relay team handing off the baton to the next runner. Only in the home the transition is made gradually and has significant overlap.

A mother prepares her son to identify with his father, in a process that will eventually result in the son's identifying more with Dad than with Mom. The son never severs his connection with Mom. Dad is an additional ingredient. But a time does arrive when the son's bond to his mother will be overshadowed, and his allegiance will shift from her to another significant woman in his life: his wife...and the mother's daughter-in-law. This important relationship is what this book is about.

$\mathcal{A}$ Report from the Trenches

Years ago a couple came to me for counseling. Jean, the wife, described the problem this way:

"Arthur's mother is our major problem. He is tied to her apron strings—but tight. I tried to be very nice to his mother when we were first married. But she never did like me. In fact, one time she came right out and told me that she didn't believe that I was the right woman for him and I never would be.

"The truth is his mother spoiled him rotten. She waited on him hand and foot. She was from an old-fashioned family, and she got all of her satisfaction from cooking and housekeeping. She ran the house and Art's father was as visible as a ghost! I don't keep house very well, and I admit it. But she didn't have to come over and pick things up after me as she did. It made me so mad I screamed at her and told her to get out. And do you know what? Art didn't even take my side!

"As a matter-of-fact, I think that's what hurts the worst. I can sometimes abide his running over there all the time, but I can't stand the fact that he doesn't stand up for me. He never says anything to his mother in my defense. He never talks back to her at all.

"She keeps working on his emotions, even more so now that his father has died. She makes him feel that he ought to come and see her every day. He goes over there at least seven or eight times a week. If I try to make him promise not to, he just lies to me and goes anyway. I've caught him at it.

"I want to move away from his mother. But he went and bought a house about a block from her place last year. When he did that, I almost left him.

"One time, when we were first married, he took a good job down in Atlanta. Do you know how long we stayed down there? Two months! He just couldn't stay away from Mama. He'll tell you all sorts of reasons why we came back: It was a poor job, we didn't like the area, and his boss was impossible to work with. But those weren't the real reasons at all."

Then Art shared his account of the situation:

"Jean is just jealous of my mother. She doesn't even want the children to have gifts from Mother. Jean is lots younger than Mother, and she could at least try to understand how Mother feels, now that her only son and her husband are both gone. Jean could end this marriage problem any time she wanted to by just acting decently to my mother. But she won't.

"Jean is a lousy housekeeper. I think she'll tell you that herself. And really, that's part of the problem. Jean knows she should pick things up, but when Mother comes over here and does it, she begins to boil. That's really what started all the trouble.

"I know Jean says she wants me to take her side, but what it amounts to is that she wants me to punish my mother as a demonstration of my love for her. She has said it almost that way. What am I supposed to do—castigate my mother because she's trying to help? I can't do that.

"I've tried to make things as easy as I can for Jean. I used to ask her to go with me to Mother's, especially on the holidays. But now I don't even ask anymore. Every once in awhile I take the children by myself. And then does Jean scream! She says my mother tries to turn the children against her. Actually, all Mother does is give them a little loving care, which they rarely get at home. Anyway, I don't go down to Mother's so much myself anymore.

"To tell you the truth, Mother has been a big problem for me all my life. Since I was the only child and her only real interest, she expected a lot of attention from me. I know I feel obligated to help her. Who else is there? You just can't tell her to curl up and die. But Jean doesn't understand this. Her own mother is an independent type who can take care of herself. She tells Jean off regularly, and Jean seems to respect her for it.

"I don't know what I'm going to do. My life is miserable this way. Jean wants me to move way across town, and in some ways it might be a good thing, though I would never admit that to her. On the other hand, it might just increase the time I had to be away from home, because I know I can't ever abandon Mother altogether."

Reflecting on This Chapter

1. What are you teaching your son about what it means to be a male? (Or, if your son is grown, what did you teach him about masculinity?)

2. What are you teaching (or did you teach) your son about what it means to be a female?

3. How do you feel about being a woman?

4. How do you feel about men in general?

5. How were you shown love as you were raised? Through verbal responses, food, touch—conditional or unconditional?

6. Which of these methods do you use to demonstrate love to your son?

7. Did you or are you teaching your son to be proud about being a male?

8. Do you want your son to be the same as or different from his father? How do or did you convey this?

9. In what way have or are you encouraging your son to be who he uniquely is, and to develop his spiritual giftedness?

10. Ask your husband to reflect on the following questions. Let him know that you are seeking information, and also hoping to discover if you can improve your relationship with him in any way. Let him know that your intention is not to react to, debate or argue over any of his responses—least of all to criticize his mother. Rather, you will just listen to him or read his responses for your own insight and understanding.

    a. What do you feel are/were your mother's positive qualities?

    b. What do you feel are/were your mother's negative qualities?

    c. How did you feel about your mother when you were a child through age 10?

    d. From ages 11 through 20?

    e. From 21 through 30?

    f. At the present time?

    g. What emotions did your mother express openly? How did she express them?

    h. Describe how you and your mother communicate(d).

    i. What was the most pleasant experience you had with your mother?

    j. What was the most unpleasant experience you had with your mother?

    k. What is/was your mother's goal in life?

    l. In what ways are you like your mother?

    m. In what ways are you different from your mother?

n. How do you feel your mother influenced your choice of a woman (women)?

Notes

1. Jean Lush and Pamela Vredevelt, *Mothers and Sons* (Grand Rapids, MI: Fleming H. Revell, 1988), pp. 23-24.
2. Ralph G. Martin, *The Life of Lady Randolph Churchill* (New York: New American Library, 1969), p. 164.
3. Ken Druck, *The Secrets Men Keep* (New York: Doubleday and Co., 1985), p. 161.
4. Darrel Gates, *Chief* (New York: Bantam Books, 1993), p. 124.
5. Robert Bly, "Men's Initiation Rites," *Utne Reader* (April-May, 1986), in Carol Staudacher, *Men and Grief* (Oakland, CA: New Harbinger, 1991), p. 88.
6. Staudacher, *Men and Grief*, pp. 37,90.
7. Michael Reagan with Joe Hyams, *Michael Reagan: On the Outside Looking In* (New York: Kensington, 1988), p. 7.
8. Ibid., p. 8.
9. David Stoop, *Making Peace with Your Father* (Wheaton, IL: Tyndale, 1992), pp. 26-27.
10. Jal Tanenbaum, *Male and Female Realities* (San Marcos, CA: Robert Erdmann Publishing, 1990), p. 26.
11. Judith Balswick with Lynn Brookside, *Mothers and Daughters Making Peace* (Ann Arbor, MI: Servant Publications, 1993), p. 67.
12. Ibid.
13. Stoop, *Making Peace with Your Father*, pp. 21-25.
14. Don Elium and Jeanne Elium, *Raising a Son* (Hillsboro, OR: Beyond Words Publishing Co., Inc., 1992), pp. 19-27.
15. Prentice Tipton, "The Crisis of Black Manhood," *Pastoral Renewal* (March 1987), p. 4.
16. Ibid.
17. Bobbie Reed, *Single Mothers Raising Sons* (Nashville, TN: Thomas Nelson, 1987), p. 80.
18. Jo Brans and Margaret Taylor Smith, *Mother, I Have Something to Tell You* (New York: Doubleday and Co., 1987), p. 85.

19. Balswick with Brookside, *Mothers and Daughters Making Peace*, p. 46.
20. Lush and Vredevelt, *Mothers and Sons*, p. 46.
21. Paula J. Kaplan, *Don't Blame Mother* (New York: HarperCollins, 1989), pp. 98-99.
22. Druck, *The Secrets Men Keep*, pp. 175-181.
23. Ibid., p. 81.
24. H. Norman Wright, *Holding on to Romance* (Ventura, CA: Regal Books, 1992).
25. Druck, *The Secrets Men Keep*, pp. 181-182.
26. Ibid., p. 83.
27. Ibid., pp. 189-190.
28. Ibid., p. 206
29. R. Scott Sullender, *Losses in Later Life* (New York: Paulist Press, 1989), p. 68.

chapter
2

#
Memories
of Mom

MOTHER.

What image comes into your mind as you say this word? Close your eyes and let your memories create your thoughts and feelings. Is it a warm, cozy, loving image? For many it is.

What about your husband's image of his mother? What about your *son's* image of his mother? What would they say? Over the years, I have asked men this question in various ways, such as, "What do you feel are your mother's positive qualities?" Here are some of the responses I have received:

1. She is kind and sensitive, loves her family and is very giving.
2. She is organized, prompt, thrifty, committed.
3. Mother is dedicated to and in love with Jesus Christ. She is loving, she is easy to get along with for almost anyone, she will do almost anything for her kids.

4. She is kind, forgiving, loving, understanding. Makes me feel that I can tell her anything.
5. She is industrious, hardworking, determined, honest, merciful and loving. Mom is a Proverbs 31 kind of woman. She reads a lot of books and is wise. Mom is remarkably nonprejudiced and tolerant of another's point of view.
6. Mom is aggressive, hardworking, never gives up, always keeps going, softhearted, strong-willed.
7. She loves us more than any child could ever want, would give us the shirt off her back or to anyone that would need it. Strong faith in the providence of our Lord. Lived her life for her children and husband, is generous, self-sacrificing, great mother—is wise in the behavior and skills in raising children.

But to others the word "mother" creates stained visions. Some mothers are martyrs or critics or punishers or invaders. The reaction of some sons may be painful, rejecting and protective. Here are some of the statements I have received over the years from sons in response to the question: What do you feel were the negative qualities of your mother?

1. She's stubborn, she smokes too much, she doesn't like people very much.
2. Mom can be a little moody at times. Although she has a lot going for her, I feel she is not as optimistic and happy as she could be if she would count her blessings more readily and worry less.
3. Talkative, always criticizes and puts down my dad in front of children.
4. Pushes her beliefs on others; lazy, neglects motherly and wifely duties.
5. Worked too much and spent little time with the family; verbally and physically abusive.
6. She puts too much pressure on herself to entertain guests/friends/out-of-towners. This results in a lot of tension when I want to have people over from out of town.
7. Not encouraging enough; was always saying we could do better.

Great Expectations

We have high expectations for mothers. Motherhood has been seen as a sacred and exclusive child-rearing role. But the view that mothers were expected to make children the focus of their lives didn't take root until the early nineteenth century. By the twentieth century, our society had define motherhood as a mandate from heaven, although it insisted on the right to define it in the culture's own terms. In 1905 in a speech before the National Congress of Mothers, President Theodore Roosevelt said, "As for the mother, her very name stands for loving unselfishness and self-abnegation, and in any society fit to exist it is fraught with associations which render it holy."[1]

A mother's duty was defined for her. *She* (not the father) was responsible to raise their children into law-abiding, God-fearing citizens for the good of family and our country. She received messages that *her* guidance and vigilance was vital, and that one slip could scar a child forever. *She* was the parent who was held most accountable for how her children turned out.[2]

Heaven *does* have a mandate for motherhood; but heaven's Ruler has the right to define what that means, even if it is contrary to society's definition. Our culture has offered several inadequate responses to the mandate for mothering. By identifying them, mothers can raise motherhood to a healthier level of functioning—and in the process, bequeath to their sons (and daughters) healthier ways of living and relating to others.

Mother as Doormat

A 40-year-old son described one negative pattern for me. He said, "I wish my mother had some strength. Everyone, including me, walked all over her. It's like we wiped our feet on her. She was a doormat. I feel bad about it but at the same time I'm angry about it, too. I wanted to see some show of strength. Mom seemed so pitiful and so dependent. It's really colored my relationship with the women in my life."

A mother like this is usually a woman who is uncertain and inse-cure. She seems to have no resistance, no strength to cope with the pressures and adversities of life. Often she is like a sponge, soaking up the moods of those around her.

weak and passive mother invites her son to become a nurturing parent to her because she functions like a needy child. But children cannot handle adult problems.

Women Without a Self

One therapist described doormat women as "deselfed" women. They're unable to defend themselves. They ignore their own needs, and punish themselves instead of meeting them. They feel that what-ever goes wrong in their lives is their own fault. They've learned to be both a judge and a jury, and their only verdict is "Guilty!"

A mother like this is convinced that "I'm unworthy."[3] She is seen as pathetic and submissive, rather than angry. But, oh, is she angry! Family members who are the most self-sacrificing often turn their anger back toward themselves and are the most likely to develop depression and other emotional problems.

Another man said to me in counseling, "I wish my passive-sub-missive mother had learned how to be strong. If only she had devel-oped some influence or power!" He was surprised when I said she had plenty of power, and controlled him quite well. When a mother gives up being dependable and strong, she actually gets other family members to fill in for her. Thus, the other members of the family help to keep her a doormat. A son learns how to cope and obtain his emotional nourishment elsewhere, because Mother always seems to be depleted. He also learns how to rescue his mother from herself or from an overbearing or abusive husband.

When the Child Is the "Parent"

If Mother gives up her adult role, she deprives her son of a strong maternal example. And if the father is abusive, no one is left to protect the son. Furthermore, a weak and passive mother invites her son to become a nurturing parent to her because she functions like a needy child. But children cannot handle adult problems. A son may want to be what she wants him to be, or thinks she wants him to be, but he can't. This unhealthy role reversal can generate lifelong anger and guilt.

Such a mother may rely on her children to fill the vacuum of neediness she feels internally. This is a form of emotional abuse or emotional incest, but it is done in such a way that it's not easily identified. Hopefully, the son learns how to protect himself from the mother in this regard.

When a son who has a doormat mother reaches adulthood, he faces several options. He may continue to rescue his mother even after he's married, or he may move as far away as possible to free himself from the bondage. He could be drawn to a woman who is similar, in the hope of changing her. Or, more than likely, he will look for a strong woman.[4]

The Dependent Mother

Tim and Judy came for counseling after only eight months of marriage. Their major adjustment issue had to do with how Tim reacted to Judy's behavior and her desire for intimacy. Tim said:

"I was so close to my mother when I was raised I think I was a replacement for Dad. She got her needs met from me, and I was uncomfortable with that. It wasn't sexual, but it felt incestuous. It was too intimate. So when Judy wants to get close, I have this reaction of, 'Whoa, slow down,' and I begin to retreat. I know up here in my head that she isn't my mother, but my emotions respond as if she were. I don't want to be this way, but I'm not sure I know what to do."

If a son has to rescue his mother, the power and importance he feels may become something he doesn't want to give up as an adult. He may want to continue to manage other people in his life because it helps to overcome hidden feelings of inadequacy and helplessness.

There is another side to this, however. If Mother is this dependent on her son, what does it teach him about women? If he was frightened and overwhelmed by his mother's needs, any time he sees another woman in pain or express dependency, he may be repulsed or turned off. If he felt inadequate with his mother, he certainly doesn't want to repeat this with a dating partner or wife.

Because such a son goes into adulthood having so many needs unmet, he may expect women to meet these intense needs. But because he may be emotionally handicapped, he can't understand why no woman can satisfy his neediness. His pent-up anger could come out in abuse. Now he retaliates for what he didn't receive from his mother.[5]

Mother the Suffocator

Jim, a man in his 40s, had an interesting but repetitive and obvious dream. He described it for me:

"Several times a month I have this dream. I've had it for years. It's somewhat terrifying. I feel as though I can't get my breath. I feel like I'm suffocating in my dream, like I'm being smothered. And it's the same person standing there time after time with a pillow in her hand:

Mother. I guess it is kind of obvious, isn't it? Yeah, it's true. I felt and still do feel smothered by her. And it's a Catch 22 case again. If I don't conform or show appreciation, I get the old martyr routine. And even though I know better, it still works."

Mothers Who Give Too Much

Some mothers are suffocators. They do it through giving and doing far too much. I've seen them spend hours typing their son's papers, and working overtime so their son could have the best motorcycle or car. If the son is too young to have a car, I've seen mothers stand by willing and available to take him anywhere, anytime.

Although a suffocator appears to be giving, nurturing and loving, it is actually overkill. When suffocation occurs, life stops. The air that is so necessary for living is cut off. Furthermore, the mother does not give too much and do too much just for the good of the son. There are payoffs for her.

A mother may have a limited life because she does too much for her son. She may vicariously live through what he accomplishes. And she has her own unique ways of letting others know her part in the success.

She intrudes into everyone's business and ends up convincing them that she is the only one who knows how to handle the issues or solve the problems. In this way, she also keeps her son tied to her, for he has learned the message that Mother is the great provider.

They Keep Doing and Doing and...

Suffocators don't know when to stop giving and doing. They deprive a son of the opportunity to learn to be strong and independent. They are always trying to fix things and make everything better.

Instead of saying, "Let me show you how to do this and then you'll be able to do it yourself and won't need me to do it for you," she keeps doing and doing and doing. And she likes him to want her to do for him. Unfortunately, she is just enabling his dependency.

When he gets married, she may have helped to create for his wife a man who never grew up. This has been characterized as the Peter Pan Syndrome. By violating healthy boundaries and squelching their sons' independence, suffocating mothers have created 30-, 40-, and 50-year-old men who are still tied to their mothers. And naturally, if the son doesn't show appreciation and tells Mother to stay out of his life, he has a martyr on his hands.

If the mother's influence is very strong, she can end up with a son who is spoiled and narcissistic, or extremely fearful and insecure. She may also shape a son who is unable to handle the normal frustrations of life. This often leads to a feeling of entitlement—the son wants everything given to him, and feels he deserves it.[6]

What may be worse is that he may become a misogynist—a woman hater—because of his mother's overprotection and overcontrol. Women haters then take it out on their wives as well as other women in their lives. They respond to women by using abuse and control. They yell, bully, threaten, use verbal attacks, ridicule and criticize, just for starters. In Christian homes they use God or the Bible to justify their verbal attack as "correction."

The Passive-Aggressive Male

The suffocating mother is often implicated in fashioning one of the most frustrating types of adult men—the passive-aggressive. This is a person who expresses his aggression in a passive way. He doesn't challenge and resist directly, but indirectly and covertly. He may think of himself as weak, and believe that passivity is the only way he can relate to those whom he perceives as more powerful. He misconstrues personal relationships as power struggles, and sees himself as powerless. The difficulty is that this type of behavior will tear apart relationships that ordinarily would survive and be healthy.

The passive-aggressive male is one who is afraid of dependency and thus tries to control others.

He is afraid of intimacy and may create conflict to create distance.

He is an obstructionist, saying he will do something for you but he won't say when, and is deliberately slow to comply if he does at all.

He sets up ongoing chaotic situations, and his life is characterized by unfinished business.

He tends to feel victimized, so he sets himself up as an innocent victim.

He is adept at making excuses and lying, which can include withholding significant information.

He procrastinates and dawdles, is chronically late, selectively forgets, uses silence, doesn't hear and sulks. He is good at giving ambiguous messages full of phrases such as, "Maybe we can..." or "Perhaps...." After he's given you an answer, you still don't know if he said yes or no.[7]

Such men are a frustration in interpersonal relationships. Some boys exhibit this tendency at an early age. Many passive-aggressive men come from homes where a mother had high expectations, had to know everything that was going on, was strong willed, overrode her husband and overinvested herself in her son emotionally.

I heard the story of one mother who pinned her son's blankets to the mattress pad at night to keep him from falling out of bed until he was five years old. As an adult, anytime he felt or perceived that he was going to be trapped by a woman, he would leave.

The passive or absent father is just as often responsible for this problem because he is a phantom father. In such cases, where is the male model with whom the son can identify?[8] (If a passive-aggressive man is involved in your life in some way, I would highly recommend reading *Living with the Passive-Aggressive Man* by Scott Wetzler.)

The Martyr

Some mothers may be what John called "different." He was hesitant to use any other terminology, although his tone and nonverbal communication said volumes more. He said, "I've finally figured out why

I'm so confused by women and seem to misunderstand them so much. I can't seem to relate to them well since I project Mother's face onto them. I'm always off balance. When I was growing up, and even now, Mom was usually a martyr, and then if that didn't work she became a dictator. She kept switching back and forth, depending upon how my brother and I responded."

A mother who is a martyr or a dictator maintains control over her son no matter what his age by making him feel responsible for her problems or distress.

"Is This the Thanks I Get?"

If Mom plays the role of a martyr, her son will hear crying, sulking and constant complaints about her health that are somehow tied into caring for her son. A martyr mother is adept at making others feel guilty if they go against what she wants. Some of the more common statements you can expect to hear are, "Look what I do for you!" "You don't care about anyone else but yourself." "I give up so much for you and this is how you show your gratitude?" "I just wanted you to have all the things I never had, but you don't seem to care about what I've done for you." "The only reason I stuck it out with your father was because of you, and now I wonder if it was worth it." "I hear you're not coming to visit me this year. I hope you enjoy wherever it is that you're going." "Don't you have a phone that works anymore? I never hear from you."

A martyr mother sends the degrading message that who you are hurts her. So a son begins to accumulate a load of guilt that he may carry into adulthood.

Martyrs are also skilled at giving double messages. "I only want what's best for you, but I don't understand why you have to move to Chicago." "It's your decision, and I'm so glad you've grown up enough to make them; but if you would listen to me...."

One 55-year-old man said, "My mother still calls us twice a day, once at home and once at work. It's 2,000 miles away. She complains about the phone bill each month, and says if we lived closer to her it would save her money and be better for us as well. She expects us to come there each year for vacation, or she wants to come here. Either way, our ears and emotions need a rest when it's over."

This man also went on to say, "As long as I can remember, I couldn't even breathe without Mother telling me again and again that I could do it better if only I did it 'her' way. Control, control and more control! I still hear her voice playing over and over like a broken record.

"She reminds me of a hovercraft. She told me what to eat, what to wear, what TV programs to watch, where to go to school. I did put my foot down in two areas, though. I drew the line at her telling me when to go to the bathroom and whom to marry! I've been punished for that last decision for years."

A mother's calling is to relinquish her son to eventually be on his own. The best step she can take is to validate his quest for independence and encourage the separation process. This step will help him throughout his adult life. A son will have confidence about himself and his abilities if his mother has allowed him to establish his own identity, take risks, make mistakes and discover what he can learn from the experience.[9]

The Dictator-Critic

Unlike most martyrs, a dictator mother is direct and open about her control. She uses fear and intimidation through angry outbursts. John's mother was unique since she vacillated between being a martyr and a dictator, which kept him off guard. Usually a person sticks to one pattern or the other. I've worked with both styles, and both have control as their purpose. By using threats of emotional or physical trauma, a mother can create inner terror within her son. Sneers, looks of silent contempt, glares or hand gestures usually are the weapons of choice.

Instead of saying, "Look what you do to me," as a martyr does, the dictator says, "Look what I'm going to do to you." Their statements are direct. "Don't be so sensitive, act like a man!" "How could you be so dumb? Listen to me." "I don't care that you're married. You're still my son and you listen to me." "You do it because I told you to and that's it!" "I don't trust your father and I don't trust you. You've always been a liar."

The statements a son hears from a dictator-mother are toxic, and are often considered emotional abuse. They're also a direct contradiction of the teaching of Scripture:

> Even in laughter the heart is sorrowful, and the end of mirth is heaviness and grief (Prov. 14:13).

> A gentle tongue [with its healing power] is a tree of life, but willful contrariness in it breaks down the spirit (Prov. 15:4).

> He who covers and forgives an offense seeks love, but he who repeats or harps on a matter separates even close friends (Prov. 17:9).

> Death and life are in the power of the tongue, and they who indulge it shall eat the fruit of it [for death or life] (Prov. 18:21).

> Do not judge and criticize and condemn others, so that you may not be judged and criticized and condemned yourselves. For just as you judge and criticize and condemn others you will be judged and criticized and condemned, and in accordance with the measure you deal out to others it will be dealt out again to you (Matt. 7:1,2).

> But the human tongue can be tamed by no man. It is (an undisciplined, irreconcilable) restless evil, full of death-bringing poison. With it we bless the Lord and Father, and with it we curse men who were made in God's like-

ness! Out of the same mouth come forth blessing and cursing. These things, my brethren, ought not to be so (Jas. 3:8-10).

Still Connected

Growing up in a dictator atmosphere leaves its own legacy. The memories and feelings seem to last forever. Ted, a 27-year-old man, reflected the common effects of having been raised by a dictator mother. He internalized the guilt and intimidation so well that he continued to pressure and punish and control himself with much more intensity than his mother ever did. He felt that no matter what he did, it was never good enough. And he felt responsible for any problems his mother experienced.

Whenever Ted came for counseling, and his mother was depressed or angry, his emotional state would make it apparent. At 27 he was still connected to her. He described a scenario that had occurred each year over the past five years. Each December his mother would call and tell him that she was coming to visit them at Christmas and would arrive at a specific time at the airport. It was usually during the middle of the workday, but she wanted Ted to pick her up and not his wife. That too was a major inconvenience.

Every time this happened, Ted's voice would register surprise and disbelief that she was coming. This just opened the door for her reaction. "You don't want me to come. I'll just stay home by myself this year." "You can't get off work to pick up your sick mother from the airport? I can see you really care about me." "You remind that wife of yours what I need to eat at breakfast. It would be much better for all of you if you started eating right."

Naturally, every visit was traumatic. Ted wasn't yet ready to disconnect from his mother and establish healthy boundaries. The inner pain and punishment were still too great. He was caught in the common trap of being either victimized by her or ending up rescuing her in some way from her self-pity. This is the case with so many sons.[10]

Grenade-Launching Moms

A pattern of mothering that implants a sour taste in the life of a son is the critic. Women like this are adept at discovering both apparent and hidden flaws. Some of them have the ability to throw a verbal hand grenade toward you, then step aside before it explodes and devastates you. Her son's friends may be present, but it makes no difference to her. She cuts and dissects. Some do it through sarcasm and caustic humor. But unfortunately, the laughter is *at* the son rather than *with* him. They may get other people to laugh as well, making an even higher price for the son to pay.

Many critic-mothers are frozen in terms of being demonstrative. When their son reaches out for a hug or embrace, they pull back and come up with some reason why they don't respond—usually it's because of some alleged problem or defect with their son.

I have run into these critical mothers before. They have this need to be in charge, but they don't have the ability or credentials.

I have talked to several men who shared the same story about the women they dated: no matter who it was, Mother would find fault. Their mother had a list of qualifications that made it impossible to find any candidate.

Victoria Secunda gives a fascinating description of the critic:

> The Critic is a woman in a state of constant dread, like a fugitive on the run—she is terrified someone will discover that she is really as unworthy as she accuses everyone else of being. The zeal with which she demeans her children is a desperate attempt to salvage, by comparison, some small shard of self-esteem. She conceals her tremulousness behind a wall of barbs, and digs, and nagging.[11]

Secunda goes on to suggest that such behavior is symptomatic not only of a battering mother, but of the psychologically battered "child" within the mother.

Dr. Jane B. Adamson writes:

> She hides her dependency, her deep need of people, under an independent, critical façade. She deprecates others to avoid revealing how much she needs them; such an admission would expose her once more to the danger of exploitation and/or abandonment.[12]

And of course the trouble always lies elsewhere in the eyes of the critic. Being either unable or unwilling to break out of her controlling and critical behavior, she is "stuck" there. If she were to change, she would be vulnerable to the same kind of attacks she makes on others.[13]

Some critic-mothers have loud and intense personalities. They yell and scream and fight with everyone in the house. Their bombastic behavior helps hide their insecurity and hurt, so no one can see the underlying reasons that drive them to attack others and keep them at a distance.

What's Wrong with This Picture?

Now that you have read about several negative patterns of mothering, one other pattern is also difficult to label. But consider the characteristics. Danger and difficulty lurk ahead for a son and his future wife if in his childhood his mother:

- Conveyed to her son the feeling that he was the reward for all the unnamed marital pain she had to endure in her life.
- Smothered her son with praise and affection.
- Taught her son that when he became an adult he would do great and wonderful things for her.
- Protected him to the extent that she never permitted him to experience frustration.

- Filled his mind with the misinformation that everyone else would allow him to do what he wanted because he was going to do something highly significant in life.
- Discouraged her son from making his own decisions but rather, encouraged him to seek her insight and approval regardless of the importance of the decision.
- Never punished him physically but used a variety of subtle techniques.
- Led him to believe that because of what he would accomplish in life he couldn't possibly be interested in girls.
- Created the belief that she would do whatever he needed, and that mother and son would always be together in life.
- Provided erratic kinds of punishment.
- Sometimes wanted physical affection, but at other times pushed her son away.
- Led him to believe that she had total power over her son's life, and that he owed her everything since she was his provider.
- Let him know in a variety of ways that meeting his basic needs was a major burden for her.
- Played the martyr, and expected and extracted sympathy from her son for this.
- Taught him he owed her now and in the future for all she had done for him.
- Showed fear and anger when her son showed signs of having a close relationship with others.

All of these responses come from mothers who try to make their son feel that only he can make her happy—which is too much of a responsibility for even an adult to bear.

If a son grows up under these conditions, some fairly predictable traits or tendencies will develop—characteristics that will influence his adult life and affect his interaction with women. He may become totally dependent, mistrust his decisions, expect everything to be done for him and expect women to give him what he wants. Such men are likely to have ambivalent feelings about women, seek a woman like

Mother, both fear women and try to dominate them, feel unworthy and doubt their ability to make value judgments about women and relationships with them.

What is wrong with this picture? It is a blueprint for developing what is commonly known as a "mama's boy."

The Perfectionist Mom

Another kind of frustrating adult son is the product of a mother who is a perfectionist, and who holds the unrealistic expectation that her children ought to be perfect. These mothers are terrific faultfinders. They seem to have an insatiable need to point out the defects of their son. They are always looking at him through a critical lens and pointing out what he did or did not do, what he said or did not say, or what he might or might not do in the future. Even the most insignificant errors or defects are quickly exposed and corrected.

Perfectionist moms who are challenged about their faultfinding often respond defensively, "I'm just trying to save him from some painful mistakes later on in life." But the pain the child experiences from consistent criticism and correction often outweighs the benefits.

Any failure of the son of a perfectionist mother becomes the trigger for verbal attacks and pressure from Mom. Unfortunately, the son often becomes the scapegoat for the mother's own failure to be perfect.

Because the son can't live up to Mother's expectations of perfection either, he often becomes a procrastinator. His fear of failing to do things perfectly for Mom will prompt him to postpone the actions for which he will inevitably be criticized. The more he procrastinates, the more overwhelmed he feels by the pressure to perform. Soon he is immobilized by his lack of perfection, and gives up. (For additional information about perfectionism, see *Hope for the Perfectionist* by David Stoop [Thomas Nelson Publishers], and *Freedom from the Performance Trap* by David Seamands [Victor Books].)

Faultfinding is not always verbal. A sneering look, a frown or a condemning gesture also convey displeasure. Nonverbal put-downs are often difficult for a son to interpret. When a mother snaps impatiently, "You still didn't pick up all the toys in the yard," at least the

Silence is the classic form of control, punishment and criticism in a dysfunctional home. God did not put us into families to be silent.

child knows what the problem is. But nonverbal criticism, such as an unexplained scowl or the silent treatment, leaves the child wondering. Silence is the classic form of control, punishment and criticism in a dysfunctional home. God did not put us into families to be silent. We were created to communicate with each other.

Paying the Price of Perfectionism
Perfectionism and faultfinding are destructive to the son, to the mother herself and to the mother/son relationship.

Faultfinding deeply wounds the son. Constant verbal and nonverbal criticism says, "I don't accept you for who you are at this time in your life. You don't measure up, and I can't accept you until you do."

In more than 25 years of counseling, I have heard multitudes of men in my office cry out in pain, "My mom's criticism ripped me apart as a child. She made me feel like dirt. I never felt accepted, and I'm still looking for someone who will tell me I'm all right."

Faultfinding also wounds the mother. The wounded son becomes afraid or angry, and often retaliates through overt or covert withdrawal, resentment or aggression.

Faultfinding really does not change anyone. Though a son may appear to change his behavior in response to the criticism, his heart rarely changes. Some children simply learn to cover their rebellious attitude by showing external compliance.

Faultfinding is contagious. A faultfinding mother teaches intolerance to the son by example. Thus he learns to be critical and unaccepting of himself and others.

Faultfinding accentuates negative traits and behaviors. When undue attention is paid to a child's mistakes or irresponsible behaviors, they tend to be reinforced instead of eliminated.[14]

The Fallout from Negative Mothering

What happens, then, to a son whose mother is either a suffocator, a critic or a perfectionist? Or, at the opposite extreme, what can happen to a son whose mother abandons him (either emotionally or physically)? What are the results of mothering that is unpredictable and erratic?

A son from such a home may end up being stuck in his emotional development. When a boy's mother is suffocating him, how can he develop the maturity to make decisions for himself? When his mother is a critic, how can he develop a sense of security and feel positive about himself? When his mother neglects or abandons him or is unpredictable, how can he feel safe about the world in which he lives?

As an adult, if another person responded to him in this way he would be able to realize that *they* are the ones who have the problem, not him. But when he is a child who receives this kind of treatment from his mother, it is difficult to see that the one whom he assumes is his strength and support is actually the culprit. So he ends up seeing himself as the problem. He doesn't yet have the capability of realizing that both good and bad can be in the same person. He sees his mother as all good and himself as all bad.

All young children go through this phase of dividing life into either all good or all bad. Maturity comes when a person can see shades of gray, which, in the case of a parent, means they have both good qualities and bad, both positive and negative. Unfortunately many children grow up idealizing their parents. So who is responsible for the unloving way the parent responds? From the child's perspective, he is!

Healthy Parenting: Observing Boundaries

A healthy mother-son relationship has a balance of healthy bonding and healthy boundaries. Bonding means forming an especially close relationship. Boundaries refer to the healthy sense of separateness that is necessary in all relationships.

Intimacy and Boundaries

People in a healthy relationship thrive on intimacy. At the same time, each person within the relational unit needs clearly defined personal boundaries. "Where do I stop and you begin?" "What is my stuff and what is your stuff?" "What is my problem and what is your problem?" These kinds of concerns assume greater and greater importance in direct proportion to the closeness of the relationship, especially a parent-child relationship.

A healthy family reflects clear lines of separation between mother-son and father-son, regardless of whether one parent or two live under the same roof. Proper boundaries have been established. Many other families suffer significant difficulties because those boundaries have become blurred and broken. This intrusiveness hinders a son's emotional development.

Perhaps the best way to describe what we mean by boundaries is to call them "property lines." When Iraq invaded Kuwait in 1990, the boundary lines were violated. Our states, counties, townships and homesites are all demarcated by clear boundaries that are elaborately specified in the written property titles. Once I requested a city employee to survey my lot so I could be clear about my property lines. I did not want to infringe upon my neighbors if I built a structure or planted some trees.

I've been invaded by my mother for the past 27 years. She still tries to make decisions for me, and tells me what to do."

I remember counseling a young man who was living on his own. "Norm," he said, "when we had that conflict between those two countries and the one invaded the other, I just laughed. So the one country has been invaded for the first time in 50 years. I've been invaded by my mother for the past 27 years. She still tries to make decisions for me, and tells me what to do. She wants to know everything that is going on in my life, and she's upset now because I don't tell her much and I don't come around. But I've got to establish myself as an adult. I've made too many mistakes already because of not being encouraged to be who I was as I was growing up. I don't want to make any more mistakes, and I don't want to be overly involved with my own kids if I have any."

This young man's experience serves as a good example of boundary invasion.

Surveying the Boundaries

How can a mother know if a problem with boundaries exists? Families may exhibit several tell-tale signs.

Parents who feel abandoned when their children begin to make autonomous choices. These parents respond to autonomy in their children by conveying guilt or shame messages about the children's lack of love and loyalty to the family or to the parents.

Parents who feel threatened by their increasing loss of control over the children. These parents use anger or criticism, not guilt or shame messages, to convey their unhappiness over the children's newfound separateness.

Families who equate disagreement with sin.

Parents who are afraid of their children's anger. Parents who are hostile toward the anger of their children.

Families that praise compliance in the name of togetherness instead of praising healthy independence.

Families in which emotional, physical and sexual abuse occur. These kinds of abuse cause severe damage to the children's sense of ownership of their bodies and themselves.

Families in which the children feel responsible for the happiness of the parents.

Parents who rescue children from experiencing the consequences of their behavior.

Parents who are inconsistent in setting limits with the children.

Parents who continue to take responsibility for the children after they reach adulthood.[15]

Predictable Problems

When boundaries are not clearly established and become easily permeable, several predictable problems can occur.

Some sons never learn to say no to others because of their excessive desire to please, or perhaps from feelings of guilt and fear. Still others set boundaries where none need to be set, usually in areas of personal need. They block off their own legitimate needs, often unaware of their existence. They would feel guilty asking for what they need from someone else.

They may refuse your offer to do something for them, and become visibly uncomfortable. They can neither give to others nor receive from them. By spoiling others, and inadvertently teaching them they don't need to give in return, such people end up neglecting caring for themselves as well as showing love, care and concern for others.

Some sons have a definite problem with the word "no." They seem to be deaf to it. When others say no, it literally has no effect. They violate the boundaries of others by projecting their own responsibilities onto others. In one way or another, they get other people to take responsibility for them.

How to Mark the Boundaries

What can you do to encourage healthy boundaries? Here are a number of positive steps you can take:

Allow freedom for family members to state their opinions. Ask them what they think, believe or feel. Listen to what they say without comment or countering. Use responses such as, "I hadn't thought of it like that before," or "That is a different way of seeing it that I hadn't considered."

Make it safe to disagree without fear of recrimination. Make statements such as, "It's all right for us to have different opinions or points of view." "We may not agree, but we can both learn from sharing what we think." Be sure to avoid condemning others for their view, or using it to get back at them in a later discussion.

Encourage every person in the family to think for himself or herself, and show that you believe in his or her ability to decide. Ask questions such as, "What do you think?" or say, "You have some thoughts about this. I'd like to hear them."

Assist all family members in discovering their talents and spiritual gifts and in developing and using them to the fullest. Encourage them to read and to take classes. Expose them to new opportunities.

Allow the expression of all feelings—including anger. Acknowledge the normalcy of anger, and model healthy ways to express it. (For assistance you may want to read *When Anger Hits Home* by Gary Oliver and H. Norman Wright, Moody Press, 1993.)

Set limits with natural and logical consequences, but not by using fear or guilt. Let others know in advance what to expect in terms of privileges and opportunities, as well as any restrictions for violations.

Allow age-appropriate choices. Don't ask a 7-year-old for responses and capabilities suitable for a 15-year-old.

Respect others when they say no.[16]

Parent-Child Roles

In a healthy family, parents are expected to meet the needs of their children, but the children are not expected to meet the needs of their parents. Unfortunately, some parents burden their children with adult expectations and demands. Usually without realizing it, a mother or father may expect a child to perform and give at a level that is unhealthy and unrealistic. One such expectation is to ask their son to meet their needs.

Healthy separateness means that a mother needs to function as an adult, and a child needs to function as a child. But some parents use their children as their source of identity. They don't want to let them grow up and become independent. They want to keep them attached—never cutting the umbilical cord, so to speak.

Dr. John Townsend describes a mother who once confided to her friend about the problems she was having with her 18-month-old son. She said that she and her son had been very close ever since he was born, but that their relationship had become very difficult of late. The little boy had become disobedient and disagreeable, even throwing nasty temper tantrums. She lamented that she was going to miss her "easy baby," and feared they were on the verge of entering the "terrible twos."

Her friend's response may have thrown her a bit because I'm sure it wasn't what she expected to hear. The friend encouraged her by saying that she could certainly understand the frustration, but she perceived this new stage much differently. She called it the "terrific twos." This second woman was actually looking forward to seeing her child's personality begin to emerge and blossom.[17]

I am not sure I have ever heard anyone describe the twos as "terrific." Yet here was a mother who was joyful about her child's growth and development. She was focusing upon what was going to happen with her child, rather than upon what those changes would cost her.

When adults have difficulty allowing their children to grow up, and fail to relate to them as adults after they have reached adulthood, boundaries have been invaded and violated. By observing parent-child boundaries, mothers and fathers can teach their children how to set boundaries. By learning this crucial lesson, a son will be better able to make responsible choices later in life.

Reflecting on This Chapter

1. Talk with your husband about his memories of his mother. Remember that the purpose of this exercise is not to be critical, but to understand parenting patterns, positive or negative, that may have influenced him. (Remember also that a son can say things about his mother that a daughter-in-law can't!)

2. What "inheritance" did you and your husband receive from your parents, in the areas of:

   a. How you feel about yourself.

   b. Your attitude about school.

   c. Your attitude toward work.

   d. Parenting styles.

   e. Your attitudes toward the opposite sex.

   f. Your attitudes about God, and the Church.

3. How do both of you feel about the statement in this chapter that an adult son whose needs were not met by his mother may

expect his spouse to care for him—in effect, becoming a "surrogate mother"?

4. Discuss where both of you think the line is between protecting and *over*protecting a child. Think about this issue in areas such as his or her friends, choices about homework and play, working after school, spending allowances, spiritual choices, boy/girl relationships.

5. What are some special challenges for a single parent? What can the church do to minister to single-parent homes?

6. Much was said in this chapter about critical as well as dictatorial parenting styles. How can parents discipline children without coming across as a critic or dictator?

7. In what specific ways can you help children develop healthy "personality boundaries"—to know which is "his stuff" and which is yours, as a parent?

8. Assess your own home by using the descriptions under "Surveying the Boundaries" as a checklist:

   a. I have felt abandoned as a parent when my child began to make independent choices. (Yes___ No___)
   b. I react with anger when I sense I am losing control over my children. (Yes___ No___)
   c. I tend to equate disagreement with sin. (Yes___ No___)
   d. I am sometimes afraid of my child's anger. (Yes___ No___)
   e. I tend to value and praise compliance more than healthy independence. (Yes___ No___)
   f. Sometimes I suspect my child feels responsible for my happiness. (Yes___ No___)

g. I have trouble letting my children suffer the consequences of their behavior. (Yes___ No___)
h. I have trouble being consistent in discipline. (Yes___ No___)

Notes

1. As quoted in Victoria Secunda, *When You and Your Mother Can't Be Friends* (New York: Delacorte Press, 1990), p. 43.
2. Ibid.
3. Ibid., p. 84.
4. Ibid., p. 85-87.
5. Susan Forward, *Men Who Hate Women and the Women Who Love Them* (New York: Bantam Books, 1986), pp. 105-109.
6. Secunda, *When You and Your Mother Can't Be Friends*, pp. 113-117.
7. Scott Wetzler, *Living with the Passive-Aggressive Man* (New York: Simon & Schuster, 1992), pp. 35-37.
8. Ibid., pp. 75-90.
9. Forward, *Men Who Hate Women*, pp. 110-114.
10. Harold Bloomfield, *Making Peace with Your Parents* (New York: Random House, 1983), pp. 81-85.
11. Secunda, *When You and Your Mother Can't Be Friends*, p. 107.
12. In James J. Rue and Louise Shanahan, *Daddy's Girl, Mama's Boy* (Indianapolis/New York: Bobbs-Merrill, 1978), pp. 207-209.
13. Ibid.
14. H. Norman Wright, *The Power of a Parent's Words* (Ventura, CA: Regal Books, 1990), pp. 101-102.
15. Dave Carter, Early Hemslin, Henry Cloud, John Townsend and Alice Brawand, *Secrets of Your Family Tree* (Chicago, IL: Moody Press, 1991), pp. 172-173.
16. Ibid., pp. 173-174.
17. Ibid.

chapter
3

The Father/Son Relationship

HAVE YOU EVER HEARD THE PHRASE, "OH, HE'S JUST A CHIP OFF THE OLD block?" What the phrase is saying, essentially, is, "Like father, like son." Some sons are total replicas of their father's behavior, attitude or pattern of speech. They seem to be cast from the same mold because they have followed Dad's example. Of course other sons deliberately choose to rebel against everything Dad stood for, but even then the son still lives his life being influenced by his father.

Why are we talking about fathers in a book essentially about daughters and mothers-in-law? I'm assuming that the primary reader of this book is a woman. But your husband has been shaped in part by his mother in ways that are also often related to the father in the home. His mother's parenting style was inevitably affected both by her relationship to her husband, and by his relationship to his son.

This same complicated web of relationships affects your own style of mothering—and will affect the kind of mother-in-law you turn out to be. Certainly it is possible for a single parent to be a successful parent. God's ideal, however, is for parenting to be a partnership. It is therefore helpful for wives and mothers to understand God's ideal as it applies to the father/son relationship. (And after reading this chapter I would encourage you to ask your husband and/or son to read it if you think it would be beneficial.)

Impressions Left by a Father

What is the calling of a father? In what specific ways is a father to be involved with his son? Having a son is an opportunity to lead him to another father, our heavenly Father. A dad who is in a right relationship with God will have the greatest opportunity to be in a right relationship with his wife and his children.

I am a father of both a daughter and a son. I wish I had known 30 years ago what I know today. Part of the problem was due to the limited resources and information that were available. Today an abundance of information is available, but it still needs to be read, applied and implemented.

Perhaps the best way to start is with a strong, graphic statement of the father's importance:

> Fathers leave a lasting impression on the lives of their children. Picture fathers all around the world carving their initials into their family trees. Like a carving in the trunk of an oak, as time passes the impressions fathers make on their children grow deeper and wider. Depending upon how the tree grows, those impressions can either be ones of harmony or ones of distortion.
>
> Some fathers skillfully carve beautiful messages of love, support, solid discipline, and acceptance into the personality core of their children. Others use words and actions that cut deeply and leave emotional scars. Time

may heal the wound and dull the image, but the impression can never be completely erased. The size, shape, and extent of your father's imprint on your life may be large or may be small but it is undeniably there.[1]

Whether he wants to be or not, a dad is one of the first and most important educators in his son's life. He will either teach by example, direct words or default.

And these words, which I am commanding you this day, shall be [first] in your own mind and heart; [then] you shall whet and sharpen them, so as to make them penetrate, and teach and impress them diligently upon the [minds and] hearts of your children, and shall talk of them when you sit in your house, and when you walk by the way, and when you lie down and when you rise up (Deut. 6:6,7).

So you, my son, be strong—strengthened inwardly—in the grace (spiritual blessing) that is [to be found only] in Christ Jesus. And the [instructions] which you have heard from me, along with many witnesses, transmit and entrust (as a deposit) to reliable and faithful men who will be competent and qualified to teach others also (2 Tim. 2:1,2).

A Fallible Mentor

I think most fathers want to be admired by their son(s). And a son wants to admire his father. You see little boys trying to walk and talk like their father. And when asked what they want to be when they grow up, they say, "Like my dad." This is healthy if it is realistic. A son needs a model or mentor who is strong and yet real and fallible. It is better to be seen as a man who has strengths and weaknesses than to be placed on a pedestal for years, only to have it crumble later on.

As one adult son told me, "The reason I can admire and respect

Dad is he admitted and talked about his faults, fears and struggles as much as his strengths and accomplishments. When he was struggling, he didn't just show it, but talked about it. He told me what he learned through his mistakes. He probably never realized how much he taught me through that. Dad was an imperfect, honest, emotionally available father. I hope I can be the same."

This father taught by example, which is a vital step toward developing emotionally healthy sons. One of the goals of parenting is to have children grow up believing and feeling:

"I am capable."

"I am not perfect, but that is OK. I can learn from my mistakes!"

"I am a child of God, and He loves and accepts me as I am."

"I am able to love and be loved by others. I love and respect myself."

"It's safe to be open and vulnerable with those I'm closest to."

James Dobson and His Dad

In his book on building self-esteem in children, Dr. James Dobson lists values that lead to emotional and physical health:

> The Bible provides the key to God's value system for mankind, and in my judgment, it is composed of six all-important principles. They are: 1) devotion to God; 2) love for mankind; 3) respect for authority; 4) obedience to divine commandments; 5) self-discipline and self-control and 6) humbleness of spirit. These six concepts are from the hand of the Creator, Himself, and are absolutely valid and relevant for our lives.[2]

It is not surprising that Dobson gives credit to his father for the values that were instilled in him as a child. He wrote this tribute on the dedication page of his book:

> This book is dedicated in deepest respect to my father,

whose influence on my life has been profound. I watched him closely throughout my childhood, yet he never disappointed me. Not once did I see him compromise his inner convictions and personal ethics. Thus, his values became my values and his life charted the path for my own. Now it is my task, in turn, to be found worthy of the two little ones who call me "Dad."[3]

One of the delightful memories Dr. Dobson has of his father was his first. He describes it in this way:

Let me give you my first recollection of my father, with whom I had a notoriously good relationship, and you tell me what the meaning of it is. This is, I believe, the first time he ever entered into my life that I can recall. It was at the end of the day and my dad, who was a minister, had been at the church all day. He knocked on the front door instead of coming through it, and I was the one that went and opened the door for him.

When I opened the door, he had a smile on his face as he said, "Come with me." Then he took me around the side of the house and there was a brand new, big, blue tricycle there! It was one exciting moment. As far as surprises of my life, that one probably ranks near the top in terms of sheer delight.[4]

My Father and My Fathering

My own father did not talk very much. One day I asked him if he loved me, and he said of course he did. I knew it, but I just wanted to hear it from him.

I am an avid reader. I love to read Western and adventure novels. I grew up going to the library every week and reading practically every book in the children's section. Why? Of course, I received encouragement from Mom. But Dad, who only finished the eighth grade, read two books a week and was constantly at the library. I had a positive model.

Dad did something else for me that totally influenced my life. As a child, I did not like going to church. The Sunday School and the church service were boring and, as I realized later, quite liberal. I found every excuse possible to get out of going.

When I was 12, my dad said he would like me to go with him to a new church. We would take the new-members class together, and then join together. That started my involvement at the First Presbyterian Church of Hollywood, where I practically lived through junior and senior high school. I was eventually influenced toward the ministry by Dr. Henrietta Mears in the college department. Dad had his faults and his strengths, but who doesn't? Sons have a choice as to which ones they will focus on.

As I reflect on my father, I can't help but reflect on my own experiences as the father of a son. The reality is that this experience was not typical of most families. My son Matthew was a profoundly mentally retarded child who never became more than an 18-month-old mentally, and died at the age of 22. I missed out on a lot, but God has fulfilled some of those voids in other ways.

Fatherhood in the Psalms

If you look into the Psalms you can discover some of the roles a father has in relation to his children based upon how God responds to us. These poems portray a father as a person a son can run to for protection. He is a source of security.

> But You, O Lord, are a shield for me, my glory, and the lifter up of my head (Ps. 3:3).

> The Lord is my light and my salvation; whom shall I fear or dread? The Lord is the refuge and stronghold of my life; of whom shall I be afraid? (Ps. 27:1).

Someone who is a refuge is both available and a haven. A father is a person of graciousness and compassion:

> The Lord is gracious and full of compassion, slow to anger and abounding in mercy and loving-kindness (Ps. 145:8).

A father is also approachable:

> In the morning you hear my voice, O Lord; in the morning I prepare [a prayer, a sacrifice] for You, and watch and wait [for You to speak to my heart] (Ps. 5:3).

A father is a person who supports his children during the difficult times in life:

> When the righteous cry for help, the Lord hears, and delivers them out of all their distress and troubles. The Lord is close to those who are of a broken heart, and saves such as are crushed with sorrow for sin and are humbly and thoroughly penitent (Ps. 34:17,18).

Fathers and Feelings

Perhaps one of the most significant but neglected tasks a father has is helping his son learn to identify and express his feelings. It is a journey through uncharted waters for many dads because of their own personal struggle in accomplishing this for themselves. Fortunately, many have discovered not only how to identify and express their feelings, but the value of doing so as well. The transfer of this knowledge and experience to sons at a young age will be a valuable gift for their development in becoming fully human.

The time to begin helping a son identify feelings is when he is a preschooler. Many of a child's feelings can be scary and overwhelming for him. He doesn't know what they are or what to do with them. This is a time in which Dad can help him understand his feelings and show him healthy ways to express them.

Speaking of Feelings

The child also needs to learn that others may feel differently about the same situation. Dad can explain, "This is what anger (or fear or sadness, etc.) is." He can say, "It's normal to feel this way," and he can ask, "What does it feel like to you?"

A young son needs his father's respect for his feelings, rather than hearing the age-old myth, "Big boys don't cry." This phrase is translated by the child into the command, "Don't have feelings." A son needs a guide for his feelings, and although his mother says they are all right, he needs another male to help him begin this journey. A father can guide his son by listening to his feelings and acknowledging them. This will validate them as real. For a young boy, this is necessary because he has a limited ability to discern between what is real and what is imaginary.

A father can provide comfort when a child is sad, while not doing anything that would deny his son the opportunity to feel the sadness. A son needs his father's permission to be sad. A father can teach his son that in time his feelings will go away. He won't feel angry or sad or fearful forever. A father can say, "I've been sad before, too." He can say, "I understand. I've been afraid myself," and "I've been happy many times."

Because anger and frustration seem to be the easiest feelings for men to acknowledge, a son will benefit from the discovery that Father has feelings other than anger.

It is important to help a son develop a sufficient vocabulary to use in describing his feelings, and this is best accomplished by hearing his father using word pictures and a varied vocabulary. Perhaps having a son will spur a father on to develop such a vocabulary.[5]

Some Compliments for Dad

It is a compliment to a father when his son is able to reflect back about his dad as these three sons did:

"My dad was an open book. We knew what he was feeling. He expressed it all. Sadness, tears, happiness, excitement, anger, fear....He taught me it's all right to feel."

"My father showed his feelings in actions, but most important, he verbalized them. When he was angry, he was honest with his anger but he would admit responsibility for feeling that way. He didn't blame us for the way he felt. I've also seen him grieve. He wept when our dog died. He even cried at my wedding. But most important of all, he told me why he was crying. One of my favorite statements he would make was, 'I really feel the joy of the Lord today.' And all this came from a quiet, introverted man. I feel privileged to have him as my dad."

"Dad expressed delight by the expression on his face, sorrow by withdrawing, frustrations by being busy and involved, but love by telling me, 'You're special, Son. I love you. God blessed me when you came along.'"

Roles Fathers Play

Dr. Dave Stoop talks about the crucial role of a father's influence, in his book *Making Peace with Your Father*. He suggests that a father's role includes that of a nurturer, lawgiver, protector and a spiritual mentor. When a father nurtures a son, the son feels secure and valued and is able to bond with his dad. But he needs to see his dad approach life with competence and confidence as well. Lawgiving is not the same as being authoritarian. It means being involved in a son's life, as well as clarifying the rules and enforcing discipline. Stoop writes:

When lawgiving is balanced with nurturing, a father

helps his children learn to make decisions about right and wrong for themselves. It is not just a matter of "following orders." When it comes to rules and standards of behavior, children operate on a "show me, don't tell me" basis. They need to see morality modeled, struggled with, confronted, and dealt with realistically and honestly. A father who is comfortably balanced in his lawgiving role is able to *demonstrate* his sense of integrity and morality by the way he relates to his children, not just *proclaim* it to them.[6]

As a protector, a father especially needs to stand with his son during the adolescent years, when they are confronted by changes that can affect both the father and son. This is a time to help a child prepare himself to battle effectively with life. Being a spiritual mentor means drawing the child into the future and helping him dream realistically. It means helping a son learn to live a life of faith.[7]

Scripture on a Father's Role
Here are some Bible passages that define the role and response of a father:

To rule	1 Timothy 3:4; 3:12
To chasten	Proverbs 19:18
To correct	Proverbs 22:15; 23:13
To teach	Deuteronomy 4:9,10; 6:7; 11:18-21; Proverbs 4:1-4; 1:8
To nurture, not provoke	Ephesians 6:4; Colossians 3:21
To provide for	2 Corinthians 12:14; 1 Timothy 5:8
To encourage	1 Thessalonians 2:11
To command	Genesis 18:19
To tell	Exodus 10:2
To guide	Jeremiah 3:4
To discipline	Proverbs 3:12; Hebrews 12:6

Sadder Memories

Unfortunately, not all fathers follow the previous scriptural guide-lines. Charles Williams cites comments from a man whose experience and memories caused him to feel cheated of the influence his father might have had on him. Hopefully, this will not be true of your own son's experience with his father:

> It's not that I miss my dad. I don't. I never really knew him so I can't miss him per se. What I do miss are the things we should have shared, the things we should have done together. I watch other dads and their sons. Some-times it hurts to watch them. I wish I could have done with my dad the things they do with theirs.
>
> I wish I could have spent more time with my dad. I wish we could have gone bowling, fishing, or to a movie together. I wish we could have just sat and talked to each other. I never confided in my dad. We never talked about girls, dating, love, life, sex, or anything. My dad was a businessman at work and at home. He never had time for me.[5]

Eventually, this adult son gained the maturity not to blame his father. He recognized that his father was only human, and he allowed him to have problems, just as he saw problems in himself. And he realized that his father did not have a close relationship with his own dad, and that he lacked an adequate example of fathering.

Equally tragic is the fact that as a boy the man never saw his father show affection to his mother. As a result, the son did not learn how to relate intimately to a woman. To this day, he says, he is uncomfortable in such situations.

He says he did see his father angry—once. That was the time his dad beat him, leaving him with welts on his legs. His mother and sister had to pull his father off of him. Now, he says, although he rarely loses his temper, there is an explosion when it does occur. He closes his reflections with these moving words:

> My dad never held me. He never touched me. He never told me he loved me or was proud of me. I know he did love me and I know he was proud of me, but he couldn't tell me.
>
> I never argued with my dad. I never asked his opinion or his advice. He had zero influence on my life and life decisions, or so I thought. Now I have discovered I am just like my dad.
>
> It's too late to change things between my dad and myself. He died eleven years ago. I wish I could tell him I'm sorry and I love him. If nothing else, he was my dad.
>
> Regretfully,
> Richard[9]

Phantom Fathers

One of the major struggles for many mothers and sons is the absent or phantom father pattern. The absenteeism is seen in various ways. Here I take the liberty of citing a lengthy passage from one of my previous books, *Always Daddy's Girl:*

> Some phantom fathers spend sufficient time in the home, but their interaction with their sons is very superficial. Dad may talk a little with his son about the news, work and sports, but he never reveals very much of himself. Some phantoms are little more than walking checkbooks for their families. They pay for everything, but they are emotionally detached from everyone.
>
> Some phantom fathers appear to be "nice guys." They are easygoing, agreeable and likeable. They are consistent, stable and passive, but they don't express any of

their feelings to their family members. This dad is very cautious since he doesn't really trust his own feelings or the responses of others to his feelings. He often fails his family by tending to store up his hurts and complaints, expressing them in passive-aggressive behaviors such as silence, forgetfulness or tardiness. A son will have difficulty developing any closeness or emotional intimacy with such a father.

The classic phantom father is rarely seen. He is a devoted provider who believes that the best way to demonstrate love to his family is to give them a good life. He works 10 to 15 hours a day, six days a week, leaving little time for him to be with his family or to get close to them emotionally. Achievement is everything to him. His interaction with family members lacks substance.

This father is often called a bystander. He is a father in word, but not often in deed. He might be in physical proximity to his son, but he isn't close to him. There is a physical presence, but not an emotional nearness. Some sons feel like they are invisible to their phantom fathers. Because Dad is unaware of his son's inner struggles and desire for closeness, his son ends up feeling like an ignored shadow.

The bystanding father seems to his son to be a man with secrets, and he may exert tremendous energy trying to discover these secrets: "Is he disappointed in me? Is he fearful and full of anxiety, incapable of relating to the real world? Is he filled with such anger against the world that it is now being redirected toward me?" These secrets can become an unspoken burden upon any child.[10]

A Pale Presence

Some men are phantom fathers because they present a weak model of what a man's role is all about. They may be weak in many situations outside the home. For example, a father may not be a good provider for some reason. If the son believes this problem stems from his father's irresponsibility, poor judgment, impulsiveness, laziness, passivity or unwillingness to take risks, he may feel that his dad has little or no strength to offer him. This weakness in itself could color the boy's perception of himself.

It is important that you as a wife respect your husband's independence, and not try to dominate or control him. Often a son notices that his father is weak or subordinate in his interaction with his mother. For example, perhaps his father goes along with his wife on a wide range of decisions, including where they live, their choice of friends, how leisure time is spent, where they go when they go out and so on.

The son may see Dad lose every argument or give in to his mother again and again. He may notice that everything his mother wants is fine with his father. He shows no strong desires or preferences. Such apparent weaknesses build into the son a lack of confidence in his father, and he may look elsewhere for his source of strength. In some cases, he may be drawn to men sexually.

> A father's manifested weakness around his wife can affect his son more directly in other ways, too. A father may have punished or scolded a son, not because *he* was upset, but because his wife pushed him to do so. Or a weak father may punish his son because he is angry with his wife, but was afraid to take out his anger on her. The son thus becomes the scapegoat. If a father is weak in his relationship with his wife, a son may give up appealing to him to intervene in his interactions with his mother. He just wouldn't help, so why try?
>
> If your husband is wishy-washy, ineffective or unassertive in dealing with people, your son may believe that he won't be able to depend on him. If he is morally weak, a son learns that he can't count on him to assist him in developing his own moral guidelines.[11]

Other Ways of Being Absent

Absent fathers are a fact of life because of death, divorce, separation, disinterest or withdrawal. In any case, the absenteeism hurts.

During my 25 years of counseling, I have learned of many fathers who are absent because of preoccupation with their own activities such as work, hobbies and personal interests. Work is often a source of self-esteem and identity for them. Dad will be away from the family most of the time doing what he is supposed to be doing—working and being a good provider. But consider this from a small boy's perspective. He realizes he is not a woman. He is a small man and is supposed to be like his daddy. But Dad isn't there that much. He is

Many homes have a combination of Dad's physical absence during the day and his emotional absence during the evening and weekends.

gone, working. So all the son can do is observe Dad when he is home, and copy his actions. He can learn to fix things, and have important things to do, but he can't learn to feel what it is like to be a man unless he has sufficient time with his father.

Another reason for absenteeism is a man's own emotional handicaps from having been raised without sufficient assistance from his own father. Many homes have a combination of Dad's physical absence during the day and his emotional absence during the evening and weekends. In such a home, a son simply cannot develop the kind of close emotional bond with his father that he has with his mother. As a result, he is likely to have difficulty learning how to feel comfortable about his role as a male. His idea of what a man is, then, is based on what he *does* rather than on his feelings. He becomes like so many men, a man whose identity is not permanent, who in order to be a man, has to be excessively "masculine."[12]

Effects of Dad's Absence

Many effects of absentee fathers are seen at various developmental stages of a son's life. For example, if his father is absent in early childhood a son might:

- Remain overly connected to his mother and have difficulty developing his own identity.
- Experience insecurity over what it means to be a male.
- Fail to learn appropriate ways of expressing aggressiveness and anger, and end up becoming passive-aggressive.
- Look to other men in work settings to be his substitute father, which can lead to disappointments or remaining in an ill-suited job.

In the elementary years, some of the same possibilities occur. A son may end up clinging to his mother, or choose to avoid closeness to another female, developing a fear of intimacy with women. When he is older and working, he could expect too much of older men, or be detached and unfocused about his work.

The possible results become intensely dramatic in adolescence. A son who has an absentee father might:

- Struggle with authority and authority figures.
- Be unable to connect to a woman out of a fear of being controlled.
- Remain a perpetual adolescent in attitude and behaviors.
- Be hesitant to apply himself in school and work, and become an underachiever.
- Be out of touch with his emotions, and become caught up in drugs, gambling, or sex.[13]

Turning from possible effects of a father's absence on a son's life, what is it like to have a husband whose father was not really present in a meaningful way? As a wife, you may have observed some of these effects firsthand.

Adult sons who grew up with absentee or phantom fathers usually have one of four reactions when they are asked to describe the emotional loss they feel toward their dads.

If a man is asked, "How did you and your dad get along?" or "How close were you and your dad?" you may hear *denial* over the situation. He may say it wasn't so bad or defend the absence with a number of reasons.

A second reaction to this loss can be *anger.* When his father is mentioned, a son can be extremely explicit about the problems and mistakes his father made. Distance between the two is usually the norm, and the wounds of this relationship may have created a vacuum within the adult son. He may have an excessive level of neediness, as well as emotional overreactions.

Other reactions may be *disappointment* and *emptiness.* The son lives with regret over missed experiences and opportunities. He is left with the feeling, "My dad didn't care," although he tried everything he could to get affirmation from his father.

Yet another reaction is *assuming the responsibility and blame* for the way dad was. The adult son may feel, "It must have been my fault. I let dad down. I was a disappointment to him." A common feeling is "If only I had been...." I've seen these adult sons pushing, striving, becoming Type A personalities and workaholics, competing fiercely—mainly with themselves—thus repeating the pattern of yet another absent father in their own home.

The Prodigal Father
Charles Williams has a unique variation of the story of the prodigal son in the New Testament that illustrates what we have been discussing. It describes a prodigal father:

A certain man had a son. The father divided his living

paying his son's bills, sending him to a private school, and trying to convince him that he was doing the best he could. Everything he did was for his son—or so he said. Not many years later, the father gathered together his interests, aspirations, and ambitions, and took a journey into a far country—into a land of stocks, bonds, securities, and other such things which do not interest a boy. There he wasted his precious opportunity of being a companion, model, friend, and guide for his son.

If a father is distant, impersonal, uncaring and will not intervene for his son, the child may feel that he is unworthy of God's intervention in his life as well.

He made money, but after spending the very best years of his life he had failed to find any real satisfaction. As he aged, he became lonely and longed for genuine relationships. So he went down and joined one of the well-respected clubs in his city. They elected him chairman of the house committee, president of the club, and even sent him to Congress.

Yet no man gave him any real friendship. So when he came to his senses he said, "How many men like me have sons whom they love and understand? They seem perfectly at ease with them and really enjoy their company, yet I do not have this. I know what I'll do. I will go to my son and say to him, 'Son, I have made a lot of mistakes, I have ignored you, and I have done you wrong. I am really no longer worthy to be called your father but could you at least let me be one of your friends?'"

So he flew back home and approached his son, who was quite moved by his words. However, instead of hugging his father and accepting him back with open heart and arms, he drew back from his father and felt ill at ease with him. His father said, "Son, I know it's been hard on you, but I want to finally be close to you."

His son replied, "Dad, there was a time I wanted your companionship, attention, approval, and friendship. But I have my own life now. It's full of a lot of problems, confusion, disappointment, and fear, but it is my life and you are not welcomed into it. I can handle it myself, thanks."[14]

$\mathcal{D}$ad and the Child's Concept of God

If there is one message for you and your husband to remember from this chapter, it is this: How a father responds to his children, whether sons or daughters, will affect their perception of God.

Damaged Views of God
Consider this:

If a father is distant, impersonal, uncaring and will not intervene for his son, the child may feel that he is unworthy of God's intervention in his life as well. He finds it difficult to draw close to God because he sees Him as disinterested in his needs and wants.

If a father is pushy and inconsiderate of his son, or violates and uses him in some way, the child may feel cheap or worthless in God's eyes. He may feel that he deserves to be taken advantage of by others. He may feel that God will force him, not ask him, to do things he does not want to do.

If a father is like a drill sergeant, demanding more and more from his son, revealing no expression of satisfaction, or if he burns with anger and has no tolerance for mistakes, the son may create a harsh God in his father's image. He may feel that God will not accept him unless he meets His demands, which seem unattainable. This perception may drive the child to become a perfectionist.

If a father is a weakling, and his son can't depend on him to help or defend him, he may think God is unable to help him, or that he is unworthy of God's comfort and support.

If a father is overly critical and constantly comes down hard on his son, or if he does not believe in him or his capabilities and discourages him from trying, the son may perceive God in the same way. He may feel he is not worth God's respect or trust. He may also see himself as a continual failure, deserving all the criticism he receives.

Dads and Enhanced Views of God

In contrast to the negative perceptions many have about God, let me point out several positive qualities of a father and how they can positively influence a son's perception of God.

If a father is patient, a son is more likely to see God as patient and available for him as well. He feels that he is worth God's time and concern. He feels important to God and that He is personally involved in every aspect of his life.

If a father is kind, a son probably sees God acting kindly and graciously on his behalf. He feels that he is worth God's help and intervention. He feels God's love for him deeply, and is convinced that God wants to relate to him personally.

If a father is a giving man, a son may perceive God as Someone who gives to him and supports him. He believes that God will give him what is best for him, and he responds by giving of himself to others.

If a father accepts his son, he tends to see God accepting him regardless of what he does. God does not dump on him or reject him when he struggles, but understands and encourages him. He is able to accept himself even when he blows it or does not perform up to his own potential.

If a father protects his son, he probably perceives God as his protector in life. He feels that he is worthy of being under His care and can rest in His security.

Allowing Scripture to Shape the Image

Although pictures of God bequeathed to us by our parents have a powerful influence, we cannot afford to base our perceptions of God and our feelings about ourselves on how we were treated by our parents. Fathers and mothers are human and fallible—and some of them are also prodigals! Inadequate concepts of God based on childhood experiences need to be cleaned out of our minds and emotions and replaced with accurate beliefs about God based on His Word. All of us need to transfer the basis of our identity from our fallible father to our infallible heavenly Father.

Our Father God is the One who is consistent in His love and acceptance. Note what the Scriptures say about Him:[15]

- He is the loving, concerned Father who is interested in the intimate details of our lives (see Matt. 6:25-34).
- He is the Father who never gives up on us (see Luke 15:3-32).
- He is the God who sent His Son to die for us though we were undeserving (see Rom. 5:8).
- He stands with us in good and bad circumstances (see Heb. 13:5).
- He is the ever-active Creator of our universe. He died to heal our sickness, pain and grief (see Isa. 53:3-6).
- He has broken the power of death (see Luke 24:6,7).
- He gives all races and sexes equal status (see Gal. 3:28).
- He is available to us through prayer (see John 14:13,14).
- He is aware of our needs (see Isa. 65:24).
- He created us for an eternal relationship with Him (see John 3:16).
- He values us (see Luke 7:28).
- He doesn't condemn us (see Rom. 8:1).

- He values and causes our growth (see 1 Cor. 3:7).
- He comforts us (see 2 Cor. 1:3-5).
- He strengthens us through His Spirit (see Eph. 3:16).
- He cleanses us from sin (see Heb. 10:17-22).
- He is for us (see Rom. 8:31).
- He is always available to us (see Rom. 8:38,39).
- He is a God of hope (see Rom. 15:13).
- He helps us in temptation (see Heb. 2:17,18).
- He provides a way to escape temptation (see 1 Cor. 10:13).
- He is at work in us (see Phil. 2:13).
- He wants us to be free (see Gal. 5:1).
- He is the Lord of time and eternity (see Rev. 1:8).

It Can Be Done!

Human fathers who make the effort to be godly men who project such biblical pictures of the divine Father know a rare joy. Something of the reward inherent in fathering according to God's plan can be seen in the following letter from Bart Campolo to his father Tony:

> Everything that was a part of my childhood is slipping away into time, and all that is left of it for me to hold onto is a bunch of old photographs and my memories.
>
> Who I am is all caught up with those special things that happened when I was a kid, and I think about them a lot these days.
>
> The times that I remember best, though, are the times I spent with you. I love those memories best of all, Dad, and they're a big part of who I am. That's the whole point of these letters for me. My childhood is gone, and I will never be able to be with you the way I was with you as a little boy. I will never be that small, and you will never seem that big again. But I have my stories, and they comfort me when I am overwhelmed by the world, when I am too old all of a sudden, when I lose my sense of wonder. They are all I have of my boyhood, and the reason I

wish we had spent more time together is that I wish I had more of them now. It isn't that you didn't do enough, you see, for I would always want more. You were the king of the world back then, the imp of fun, the man with all the answers, the one who could always fix what was broken. You made life seem magical to me.

When you die, Dad, I will surely go to pieces for a while, because I still count on you more than anyone knows, but in the end I will be all right. I will have my stories, and in them I will always have part of you, the part that tells me who I am and where I came from. I only wish there was more because what there is means all the world to me.

Love,
Bart[16]

May this be a model for all those endeavoring to be a godly father to their sons.[17]

Reflecting on This Chapter

1. Discuss with your husband his memories of his father. Again, remember that the goal is not to blame, but to understand, and to discern parenting patterns you can use, or avoid, in your own home.

2. In this chapter the ideal father is described as a "fallible mentor." Do you agree with this description?

3. Can you identify with the author when he describes the limitations he experienced in relating to a mentally retarded son? In what ways does distance sometimes occur between a father and a son even when retardation isn't a factor?

4. Discuss with your husband how he feels about the fact that his children's idea of God will probably be shaped by the way they experience their human father. What limitations are there on the analogy between our earthly fathers and God as our heavenly Father?

5. Discuss with your husband how he feels about communicating feelings to your children.

6. Discuss with your husband how he feels about the letter from the man to his father, who "never had time for me."

7. Do you as a wife feel that you respect your husband's independence? Do you sometimes experience your relationship as a power struggle? What can be done to improve such relationships?

8. Do you as a wife feel that you deal with some of the effects of your husband's "absentee father"? In what ways?

Notes
1. Randy Carlson, *Father Memories* (Chicago, IL: Moody Press, 1992), pp. 13,62.
2. James Dobson, *Hide or Seek: How to Build Self-Esteem in Your Child* (Grand Rapids, MI: Fleming H. Revell, 1979), p. 171.
3. Ibid.
4. As heard on "Focus on the Family" broadcast, August 1989.
5. Frank Minirth, Brian Newman, and Paul Warren, *The Father Book* (Nashville, TN: Thomas Nelson, 1992), pp. 62-63.

6. David Stoop, *Making Peace with Your Father* (Wheaton, IL: Victor Books, 1991), pp. 60-61.

7. Ibid., pp. 55-76.

8. Charles Williams, *Forever a Father, Always a Son* (Wheaton, IL: Victor Books, 1991), p. 169.

9. Ibid.

10. H. Norman Wright, *Always Daddy's Girl* (Ventura, CA: Regal Books, 1989), pp. 99-101, adapted.

11. Ibid., p. 112, adapted.

12. Joan Shapiro, *Men, a Translation for Women* (New York: Avon Books, 1992), pp. 59-60.

13. Stoop, *Making Peace with Your Father*, pp. 103,121,142.

14. Williams, *Forever a Father, Always a Son*, pp. 15-16.

15. Adapted from Wright, *Always Daddy's Girl*, pp. 194-197.

16. Tony and Bart Campolo, *Things We Wish We Had Said* (Dallas, TX: WORD Inc., 1989), pp. 212-213.

17. Many practical resources are available to help men fulfill their calling to be godly fathers to their sons. Some of these include:

    Men Have Feelings, Too by Gary J. Oliver (Wheaton, IL: Moody Press, 1993).

    How to Be a Hero to Your Kids by Josh McDowell (Dallas, TX: WORD Inc., 1991).

    Three books by Dave Simmons (Wheaton, IL: Victor Books):

    Dad the Family Counselor; Dad the Family Coach and *Dad the Family Mentor*.

Part II

Understanding Your In-Laws

chapter 4

Establishing Freedom in Marriage

Therefore a man shall leave his father and his mother
and shall become united and cleave to his wife, and
they shall become one flesh.—Genesis 2:24

IN MY COUNSELING, I HAVE HEARD MOTHERS SAY, "WHY CAN'T I CONTINUE TO
care for my son after he's grown and married? You know, you never
stop caring!"

It is true that a mother should never stop caring, but perhaps the
best way to care is to encourage that adult son to care for himself.
This is involved in the principle of "leaving" and "cleaving" in the
above passage from Genesis.

Cleaving by Leaving

When taken seriously, the principle of leaving and cleaving helps establish healthy in-law relationships because it breaks the bondage of old relationships. You cannot fully connect in a new relationship unless there has been a full and healthy break with the previous relationship.

The Hebrew word for "leave" means "to abandon, forsake, sever, cut off." It is vivid, descriptive language designed to convey the extent of this act. It certainly doesn't mean to literally abandon and forsake one's parents. Rather, it's a message to let you know about the transfer of commitments and loyalties at a transitional time in life.

I have seen adult sons move out of their home and marry without really *leaving*. I have seen adult sons live in their own apartment but still have their parents cook, clean and bail them out financially. To leave involves far more than moving out. It means to be physically, emotionally and financially independent from one's parents, rather than retaining any vestige of dependence upon them. Of course, it must be recognized that when dependency remains, it may be because of either the adult child's or the parents' desires.

On the other hand, a man I'll call Jim was a 30-year-old son who still lived at home. But because he was independent in his total lifestyle, he had "left home" more than some who were out on their own.

It is interesting to note that two of the factors sociologists have identified as being highly significant to the success of a marriage are whether people have emotionally separated from their parents in a healthy way, and whether they have had an opportunity to live on their own by themselves before they married. If both of these conditions existed, they have a better opportunity for a successful marriage.

The initial year of marriage is amateur time for everyone—the couple as well as their parents. Everyone is a novice, trying to adjust to new roles and expectations, and to discover a new sense of balance.

Style: Your Family's or Mine?

However committed a couple may be to marriage as a permanent bond, it may have a certain tenuousness to it simply because of this newness. For many, this is a time of tension between loyalties. And if the parent-child bond was strong and healthy, the attachment to parents may feel stronger than the attachment to the new spouse. This can make the separation painful for both the parents and the adult child.

Part of the tension can be accentuated by the choice between which family pattern to follow, "your family's or my family's?" Merely analyzing whether your energy is focused on making your parents or your children happy is a statement about your priorities. It is important that all members of the cast in this play, both sets of parents as well as the new couple, make the same commitment and voice it out loud. Building the new marriage must take center stage, especially during the first year of marriage.

In-law resentment is common among newlyweds. But it is important to realize that most of it stems not from attitudes toward the in-laws but from a person's own anxiety about leaving his or her family. If a son came from a family that was very "enmeshed," he may avoid becoming close to his wife's family for two reasons. He may be tired of being in an intrusive family situation, and afraid that her family might be a replica of his own. Or he may be concerned about being perceived as disloyal by his own family.

In many cases, criticism of in-laws is often an expression of one's own frustration and anger at one's own family. I have seen several cases where a son or daughter-in-law felt torn between parents and spouse, and in turn lashed out at the in-laws to try to deny any feelings of attachment to the family of origin.[1]

Visiting: How Often Is "Often"?

One of the adjustments to be made in a new marriage is how often to have contact with parents. This is a major issue for many couples. In premarital counseling sessions I ask the question, "How frequently do you plan to call or visit your parents?" The varied responses include the following:

"I'd like to make a brief call each day just to see how they're doing."

"Once or twice a week a phone call is in order, or twice a month depending upon where we live."

"I think we ought to see them once a week at least, but my fiance thinks once a month is better. What do you think?"

"Because of where we will live, we plan to visit them once a year, and they will come our way once a year as well."

"I want to take our vacation and spend it with my parents and brothers since I won't see them any other time. But Sue doesn't see it that way."

I also ask the parents to respond to the same question about phone calls and visits. The responses I've received vary there as well. Whenever we hear the phrase, "I want them to call or visit often," it's essential that we define the word "often."

When a person comes from a close, caring family structure, this transition causes greater pain. And the assumption is, "We'll stay in touch regularly, won't we?" If the contacts are based on mutual, healthy love, mutual interests, spiritual fellowship and friendship, this is healthy. But if it's because of dependence, I see destructive overinvolvement. A newly married couple will have to work toward a balance in contacts so they don't interfere with the growth of their own marriage.

Cultural elements enter in here also. A son from one culture may believe that calling parents once a week is evidence of too much attachment, whereas in another culture it could be seen as neglect.

Purposes and Priorities

Both the parents and the married children need to consider certain questions in their contacts with one another. What is the purpose of your call or visit? What would be the result of not calling or visiting? Are any of you assuming a counseling role that would be more appropriate for another person to fill? If you're calling for advice, who would you call if you didn't have this person to turn to? Is there any way in which you are fostering dependency in your contacts? Does anyone complain to you about his or her spouse? (If so, this is inappropriate conversation.) In your relationships, whom are you seeking to please, your partner or the other family members?

No one at any age should run home to a parent; nor should a parent foster or accept their adult child running home to them after marriage. It doesn't help, but only contaminates relationships.[2]

The following questions are for both the son and the daughter-in-law:

1. Do you spend the most time at present with your spouse or your parents? (If you think this is a strange question, don't. Some spend more time with parents.)
2. Will you spend more time with your parents or your spouse in the next six months?
3. If the decision you make is in favor of your spouse, how will this affect your and your spouse's happiness?
4. If you decide in favor of your spouse, how will this affect the happiness in the relationship between you and your parents? Will it stay the same, increase or decrease?
5. If you decide in favor of your parents, how will this affect the happiness between you and them?
6. If you decide in favor of your parents, how will this affect the happiness between you and your spouse? The general rule here is that marriage partners should usually do what increases happiness between them, even if it disturbs their parents' happiness. If the parents or in-laws are disturbed by a decision that increases the marital happiness of the couple, that is the parents' problem.

The responsibility of married couples to each other involves a total commitment. This means literally "forsaking all others." This not only includes in-laws and parents, but friends, fishing companions, tennis cronies and so on, for the sake of the marriage. When a hus-

band and wife marry, they commit themselves to the task of building
a good and enriching marriage. We don't usually make lifetime commitments to friends or business associates, but only to our spouses.

Joseph and Lois Bird suggest:

> If the relationship with parents, friends, or relatives—their
> visits, actions, or influence—has a negative effect on our
> relationship with the one person to whom we have com-
> mitted ourselves, we can make no rational choice other
> than to curtail—or even terminate—contacts with our
> parents (or others). The responsibility rests on each one
> of us. If necessary we may have to take steps which could
> alienate our parents, and they may be deeply hurt.[3]

The authors go on to say that this advice is not intended to hurt
anyone, least of all one's parents or friends. It is simply a matter of priorities, and of making choices *for* the marriage, not against anyone.

How Near Is "Nearby"?

Several difficulties can arise when young married couples live close to
either set of parents. (Even more arise if you live under the same roof!)

A study made in 1984 found that 66 percent of parents age 65 and
older lived within 30 minutes of at least one of their adult children,
and contacts were frequent. About half of them saw a child every
day or two.[4]

The most common complaints mentioned about having parents
live too close were the following: They felt the parents expected too
much in terms of anything from dropping in constantly unannounced,
to having to have Sunday dinner together every week, to wanting to
clean without being asked.

Another complaint tied to living too close was complaining constantly. Some parents who lived close to their adult children tended to
call and complain when things were not going well. Adult children
made statements like, "I hear about all the aches and pains, and what

isn't going well from their shopping trip and the miserable state of the world from their two hours of news viewing."

Another person said, "When Mom calls and complains, I get the feeling she wants me to drop everything and come over and help. But I have my own wife and children now and I just can't do that." Still another responded, "I wish there were a law that when a parent calls with a complaint or negative comment they would then have to give at least two or three positive comments to balance it out."

Many adult children find that when parents live close they tend to interfere with raising their children. This is a special irritant when a husband's mother is the perpetrator. It should be expected that adult children will do things differently with their own children. If it isn't actual abuse, then grandparents should not undermine the parents' efforts. They should ask the parents' permission before telling the grandchildren they are going to take them somewhere, and they should allow the parents to be the authorities. If grandparents ask, "Could I offer a suggestion?" they should remember that their adult child has the right and the freedom to say, "No thank you," or to decide to do it their way even after listening to the suggestion.

The last complaint mentioned was that parents or in-laws who live nearby tend to be nosy about the details of their adult children's life. This included asking inappropriate questions, driving by to see if they were at home, or who else is there, and looking through cupboards, the refrigerators or the trash and making comments on what they found.

Space, Time and Authority

It seems strange that rules about boundaries need to be clarified with family members. Yet it's a way to relieve parent and in-law tensions. In an earlier chapter we talked about boundaries. Both generations need to respect proper boundaries, especially if they live within close proximity of each other. Space, time and authority seem to be the major issues that emerge again and again. Discussing these issues with a series of questions based upon the following concerns can eliminate any violations and move the relationship toward healthy interaction

Space. This has to do with the territory in your house. Both generations need to respect the other's territory. Are any areas off limits? If so, have these been stated? The most frequently mentioned are the cupboards, closets and refrigerator.

If we were in a friend's home, we would ask before opening a closet or cupboard. It works well in family relationships, too. It's not just poking around that is the problem, it's making comments and rearranging. Neither the parents nor the adult children have been called to be inspectors of the other. Respect is necessary.

I have seen adult children go to their parents' home, which is tidy and clean, and within a half hour the place looks trashed. They invade the refrigerator, eat the last piece of their dad's favorite pie and leave the kitchen a mess. That may have been their pattern while living at home, but it's no longer acceptable.

Time. Can parents or adult children drop by anytime, or is it best to call first? Are guidelines needed for phone calls? Frequency, length of call, time of day and the freedom to say, "I'm busy and I'll call later," without being offended are issues to be clarified.

Also, parents want to get together with their adult children for occasions other than being used as baby-sitters!

Authority. The issue of authority is usually tied in to issues with the children. I have actually heard grandparents say, "I'm their grandparent, and I have the right to spoil them." That's a sure way to end up not seeing the grandchildren very much! I have had many clients come in for help with these issues. The main issues center around gifts, rules and discipline. Should the parents get permission before giving their grandchildren gifts or treats? What pattern of discipline do the parents need to follow? Are the grandparents in charge of setting the rules and guidelines when they have the children, or do they follow the other generation's rules?[5]

Talking It Over

You can take some specific steps to make your in-law relationships easier. Talk together about phone calls, and let them know what to expect from you as well as what you would like from them. Why keep everything hidden?

Sometimes parents don't want their children's visits to be lengthy, especially if they end up baby-sitting with three grandchildren under the age of three. Many grandparents have said, "The good thing about being a grandparent is that we can always leave or send the grandkids home!" Talk in advance about your visits and when it would work and for how long.

Remember that some people may find any limits inappropriate and upsetting. This could be because of personality type, personal insecurity issues or social status. I have seen some mothers whose status is threatened if they don't have both the frequency and length of contact she *and her friends* believe should occur. But everyone has a preference and choice in these issues. Families might discover that shorter get-togethers are actually much more pleasant and less draining. If plans are clear from the outset, fewer misunderstandings can occur later.

Give your parents or in-laws as many opportunities as possible to see you in your adult roles in everyday life. My son-in-law is in a distinctly different profession from mine. He is a fireman, and I am always learning from him even though he is 24 years younger than I am.

When you do visit one another, become involved in the host family's activities. Endeavor to see the other person in a new context, and try to discover what you can learn from each other.

If either generation brings up a past issue, you may want to ask if that concern has occurred recently. If not, discuss how you can see one another in a different light, and the value of seeing each other as having the potential to change.[6]

Special Events: Blessing or Curse?

Many families have the tradition of getting together for special events such as birthdays, Thanksgiving and Christmas. These can be joyous times together, the only sorrow being that they come to an end, or they can be times of painful endurance and everyone wondering if it will ever end!

Toward Better Times Together

If you plan in advance by carefully evaluating the situation, you can make these experiences better, whether they are at your place, your parents' or your in-laws'. If you came to me asking how you could make the family get-togethers better, you would hear several questions directed back to you, including the following:

What do you want to have happen during the family visit or get-together?

What would you like to change about the time? yourself and your responses? the other people?

What is possible to change?

What have been the best times, and what made them that way?

An important question, but one that may raise some mixed feelings, is, Why are you getting together? What is the purpose of the event? An honest answer to these questions may relieve some pressure. I have heard responses such as:

"I miss them and want to see them."

"I'm going because my husband needs to be with them. They're getting older."

"Our children need to know their relatives."

"I'm going out of obligation. The guilt I would feel if I didn't go is worse than getting together."

"We have a wonderful time. It's a highlight of the year for us."

"I'm concerned about the upset it would cause if we tried to change anything about our gatherings, even though they do need some new life. I just go along with the rest of them."

Once you have identified why you are getting together, identify and modify your expectations. If you are prepared not to be surprised when the grandparents get upset because your children want to play video games instead of talking with them, you will be in a better position to help them accept each other's ways.

And if your mother-in-law complains about all the work and stress over fixing Christmas dinner *every year,* why let yourself be surprised and upset when she does it again? If you go to the gathering giving everyone permission to be who they are, and prepared for certain events and traditions to occur as they always have, you will be less stressed.

Also, identify how you can respond differently when you are there. Remember that you can't change severe dysfunctional patterns. I have found that most people have some things they would like to see changed at family get-togethers, but too often just complain about them rather than doing anything about them. What exactly do you want to change? Be specific with your concerns. I usually have people make a specific list of their complaints, and then write out what they will do differently. Once that is done you can make a plan on how to make it happen.

For example, very few families take into consideration personality differences. All the extroverts enjoy talking and interacting all day, and wonder what is wrong with the introverts who find ways to escape the draining interaction. If all the noise, confusion and interaction is overwhelming, create times when you can retreat in order to recover.

Some of the changes families could make is the length of the visit, where they stay, what they bring and so on. Some might think it would be enjoyable if everyone stayed at the same house, but it may be more restful to stay in a motel. It may be better to visit one family on Christmas Day instead of frantically making the rounds of three families!

Together, but Free

A man once told me, "Norm, our family visits are so predictable, I can tell you what's going to happen at every 15-minute interval. These get-togethers are so boring. I wish we could avoid them."

My response was that if he didn't care for the ongoing agenda, why not add something new! It could be as simple as putting a question on pieces of paper, putting them under the plates, and having everyone respond to the question after the meal.

What can you do about those "this-is-the-way-we've-always-done-it" traditions that are part of our background, and that sometimes bring discomfort and conflict if anyone suggests they be changed? Perhaps we can learn from the way Jeff and Jackie Herrigan expressed the problem:

> The pressure to conform is harder to avoid with family than with friends or neighbors. You love these people, you don't want to hurt them, and you know that they are not trying to meddle, but rather include you in their lives with that same love. Jeff and I might be able to agree on new traditions for us, but how would his mother feel when we told her we'd like to have Christmas dinner alone with our children next year? Would she be hurt if we preferred to get together with the family earlier in the day or on Christmas Eve? Even if she understood that we felt Christmas morning should be spent with our four young children, would the rest of the family be as sympathetic? Would they believe that we weren't rejecting them? We wanted to share some of our times with them, but our children were at an age when teaching the rules of the Monopoly game on Christmas morning was more important than getting the turkey in the oven on time.
>
> Would my parents understand if we used our summer vacation to take the children camping this summer instead of spending these two weeks with them? We honestly felt it would be good for the youngsters and for us, but could they accept that explanation without reading more into it? Would my grandmother still love me if she found out that occasionally I fed my children frozen pizza?
>
> How would Jeff's father feel if we didn't bank where he had always banked? If we chose to reject the law firm and stockbroker he had used all his life? Would he think that we had no regard for his experience and judgment,

or that we had little respect for the men he had dealt with for almost half a century? Or would he understand that we wanted younger men who might better relate to us and to our lifestyle to handle such matters? How would our older sisters and brothers feel if we didn't go to the pediatrician and the obstetrician they recommended? When Aunt Minnie came to visit, would we hide the frogs, pet snakes, and lizards the children took to bed with them because she'd be horrified? Or would we say, "We're proud of our youngsters, and this is the way we choose to live"? Would we have the guts to stand up to Aunt Minnie and hope she'd understand?

But what if she didn't understand or approve? What if none of them understood? We decided that we'd have to try to live our lives our way. We'd go as gently as we could, and tread as softly as possible through the areas that were dear to another member in the family, but go ahead we must....Jeff's mother, who I was convinced would be the most hurt by changes in family tradition, was the most understanding. "You're building something good, something worthwhile," she said, "with your own children. Don't worry about what anyone else thinks."[7]

You need to decide what is right for you. Families need the freedom to develop their own traditions. Of course, you might decide that some of the customs from your backgrounds are to your liking. But maybe you have heard of a new custom from another family that you would like to try. Perhaps you can take traditions from both sides of the family, along with some new ones you develop and use for your own family.

Changing Things, Accepting People
You do have a choice in changing your expectations in what you choose to remember about your family, and your way of responding

to the various family members. But you may be unable to change the *people* from whom you would like to receive acceptance. When

You may be unable to change the people from whom you would like to receive acceptance. When this happens, it's necessary to learn to accept their nonacceptance!

this happens, it is necessary to learn to accept their nonacceptance!

Someone who is struggling with a difficult person often bristles or becomes angry or sits back in a defensive posture when I suggest the need to accept that person. His or her perception of acceptance may involve liking or approving of what that other person does. That is not it at all.

Acceptance means giving up our dream of other people changing and becoming just who we would like them to be. After we have creatively and patiently tried everything we can think of, the other person may just be determined not to change. Some people may want to change, but they may feel incapable of doing so. Instead of fighting it, you can choose to accept their resistance or incapability and live with it.

Adjusting Expectations

I recently made this acceptance suggestion to a man who was telling me about his mother's latest phone call. Ted had initially come in for counseling because of his struggle to cope with some family issues. We talked about his relationship with his parents. Every phone conversation ended up with his being on the receiving end of negative remarks. Ted would be quiet and upset for days, which created a strain in his own family, and he would take out his anger on those around him.

In an attempt to resolve this impasse, I began asking some questions. "Ted, how often does your mother call you each year?"

"Maybe 20 to 25 times."

"How many of the calls are the way you would like them to be? How often is your mom positive, not critical, perhaps even affirming?"

Ted said, "You may find this hard to believe, but I would say maybe one phone call a year. That's all, just one. I mean it."

"So overall, how would you describe your mother over the past few years, negative or positive?"

"Negative. I've shared that with you ever since I've been coming here. She is so critical!"

"But you expect her to be positive when she calls. Is it realistic for you to expect that, given the past history you've described for me?"

"No, I guess not."

"So why be surprised when she's negative? She's usually this way, and you've survived each phone call even though it's been upsetting."

Ted actually finished what I was going to say: "So, I ought to just figure this is Mom being Mom. Why should I expect anything different at this point, unless there's some dramatic change in her life? She's who she is."

I also suggested that in his heart and mind, Ted try to give his mother permission to be who she is—to be negative at this time in her life. If he could learn to respond to her criticism in new ways, he would be better able to cope with the painful interaction. Accepting his mother as she is and giving her permission to be a certain way could significantly free him to move ahead in the relationship.

Then I asked Ted one other question: "When your mother is positive and affirming that one time during the year, do you compliment her? Do you say something like, 'Mom, thanks for being so positive and affirming today. It's good to hear you like that'?"

He sat quietly and then said, "No, I guess I never have."

All I said was, "It's worth doing. You may be surprised at the results."

Whether your long-term difficulty involves a parent, sibling, grown child, young child or spouse, perhaps a new level of expectation and a new way of thinking would help.

One man formulated a specific statement to help him become accepting: "My older brother is critical of me. I recognize that, and I'm fairly sure that he will be the next time we talk. I can accept that he's this way. I'm coming to realize that this is his cover or protection against some hurt or defeat in his life. I don't understand why. I may know some day, and then again, I may not. Right now at least, I can't expect any more than this."

Praying for Changed Hearts

Perhaps the most likely way to effect a change is to specifically pray for the person you have difficulty accepting—and for yourself, too. Ask God to begin healing this person of the root causes of the problem. And ask God to change your own capacity to accept him or her. Ask Him to give you a heightened degree of understanding and patience. Pray for Him to help you deal with the traits or responses in yourself that you do not like.

One counselee told me an amazing story. Not every situation will turn out this well, but many do. She said:

"The last time I saw my older sister—the family perfectionist and keeper of the faults of others—I simply told her that it was perfectly all right for her to attempt to be perfect and expect us to be that way. It was also all right for her to point out our faults and we would accept her doing this. But I also said that I was concerned about her, because if she was this way toward us, she was probably the same way toward herself. I told her I would be praying for her that the Lord would help her discover the root cause of her being so hard on herself.

"I concluded by saying that I was more concerned about her way of treating herself than the rest of us. She didn't say anything and I thought she was going to cry. She called yesterday and I thought I was talking to a stranger. She wasn't critical; she was actually friendly. I can't believe the change."

A person's negative characteristics often assume such a prominent position in our thinking that they soon overshadow the positive traits. Sometimes we need to get another person's perspective or interpretation of an encounter with a difficult person. A more objective observer may be able to help us identify the positives, as well as reinterpret what have always appeared to be negatives.

Flight Solves Little
Many people become exhausted in their struggle to cope with long-term relationship difficulties, including in-laws who are seen infrequently. Huge uproars and angry confrontations begin to erupt when someone does something wrong. The destructive disruption of the delicate family balance leaves everyone defensive, reacting and polar-

The decision to cut oneself off from the family can itself be a sign that you are not free at all; you may be under their influence to an even greater degree.

ized. It is not unusual for some of those involved in the trauma to decide that the relationship is not worth it. They may decide just to cut off all contact.

This kind of decision to withdraw from a painful family situation is one of the most unfortunate experiences I have encountered in my counseling.[8] Some situations may be intolerable, but too often, however, the decision to break the relationship occurs prematurely.

Despite your immediate family's need to be free to make its own decisions, it is worth making every effort possible to maintain good relationships with the extended family in order to learn to get along and to live in peace. The fact is, the decision to cut oneself off from the family can itself be a sign that you are not free at all; you may be under their influence to an even greater degree! When you react against other people and decide not to be around them, you are allowing their behavior to control you. They are still involved in your life. This is not the biblical pattern of leaving. This is fleeing.

Reflecting on This Chapter

1. Take stock of your present relationship with your in-laws or parents. If it is strained, what might you be doing to contribute unnecessarily to the situation? (Example: Do you frequently hold up your own parents' traditions as a model to your mother-in-law?)

2. What bothers your parents or in-laws most about the way your family operates? (Example: They think I'm too strict [permissive] with their grandchildren.)

3. What expectations of you do your parents or in-laws have that you could easily meet without sacrificing your independence from them?

4. Are you aware of any resentment toward them that might cause you to unnecessarily flaunt your independence from them?

5. What expectations can you simply not meet without compromising the integrity and independence of your own home?

6. In what ways could you affirm and encourage your in-laws or parents? Could this ease any sense of rejection they may feel because of your having established your own home?

7. Which of your expectations for your parents or in-laws are unrealistic?

8. What makes it difficult for you to adjust your expectations, allowing them to be themselves?

9. Write down the names of extended family members you find most difficult. Ask someone who can be objective whether they think the difficulty is real. Then write down the positive qualities of those persons. Would it be possible for you to let them know that you appreciate these qualities? Can you honestly bring them to God in prayer?

Name	Difficulty	Positive Quality

112   Establishing Freedom in Marriage

Notes

1. Miriam Arondo and Samuel L. Parker, *The First Year of Marriage* (New York: Warner Books, 1987), pp. 46-47.
2. Anne F. Grizzle, *Mother Love, Mother Hate* (Columbine, NY: Fawcett Books, 1988), pp. 143-157.
3. Joseph and Lois Bird, *Marriage Is for Grown-ups* (New York: Doubleday, 1969), p. 142.
4. Lynn Osterkamp, *How to Deal with Your Parents* (New York: Berkley Books, 1992), p. 137.
5. Ibid., pp. 137-141.
6. Ibid., pp. 135-137.
7. Jeff and Jackie Herrigan, *Loving Free* (New York: Ballantine Books, n.d.), pp. 227-228.
8. H. Norman Wright, *Family Is Still a Great Idea* (Ann Arbor, MI: Servant Publications, 1992), pp. 194-197.

chapter
5

Guidelines
for
Adult Married Children

ONE OF THE JOYS OF WORKING WITH COUPLES IS DISCOVERING THOSE RELA-
tionships that work out well after the wedding. All the planning
involved in a wedding can create stress and tension for anyone! As we
have said, in some cases the new bond can create some tension simply because it is replacing the old bonding with parents. Yet it should
also be noted that many couples discover a better relationship developing with their own parents as well as their in-laws after the wedding.

It is interesting to see how adult children can become more objective, and more understanding, of their parents after they marry. This is
an opportunity for a person to give up a dysfunctional role as they
now transition into their own marriage.

Having in-laws may also present a person with some new opportunities. In-laws can provide you with the opportunity to recreate a
family relationship in the way you would like. Because you have in-

laws, you may be able to rewrite problem scripts that existed in your own family. Having a father- or mother-in-law can provide an opportunity to create a new kind of relationship with an older adult that is not contaminated by the same problems, issues or conflicts that were experienced with a person's own parents.

ℬuilding Blocks for Relationships

In my counseling practice, I have found that certain principles of dealing with families have the best potential for building healthy relationships. These guidelines are based upon extensive interviews with married couples over the years.

Communicating Your Feelings

The first principle involves communication, and is of paramount importance for any area of family relationships. Whenever you share your feelings with either your spouse or your in-law, be tactful, sensitive and respectful.

Time after time I have seen a person raise an issue about their spouse's parents (their in-laws) that is packaged and presented in such a way that it was perceived as an attack. Naturally, the most common response to any attack is a defense.

Communication is smoother when you distinguish between facts and feelings. Too often, concerns and complaints are shared as facts rather than feelings. When you share a problem, reduce the threat on the part of the listener by sharing your feelings rather than by placing the emphasis upon the wrong you think others are doing. If your complaint is based upon what you feel, you are less likely to run into a brick wall.

If you feel your partner does not put forth much effort to get better acquainted with your family, don't label him or her as unfeeling, aloof, noncaring or selfish. Instead, share what you would like him or her to do. For example, you might say, "I really feel that we should spend more time with my family," instead of, "You never show any interest in being with my family."

If you feel ill at ease with your spouse's parents, talk about your own discomfort first, and then what you think or feel the reason for that might be. For example, you might say, "Sometimes I feel I can never please your mom. I wonder if she thinks I'm not taking good care of her son."

Time after time I have heard the concern from either a husband or wife that his or her partner changes and acts like a different person when they get together with their parents. Often this is true, but if it is approached with concern and sensitivity, this outside observation could be a benefit to the person. You might say, "Sometimes I feel as though you're walking on eggshells when we're at my folks' place," instead of, "You always put on an act over there."

Are there ever times when feelings about your in-laws should not be shared? Perhaps so, if you are irate, very resentful and punitive, or cannot tolerate them. It is probably best to spend time writing out your feelings, both for drainage and for clarity. Sometimes it helps to talk through thoughts and feelings with an outside, objective, resource person.

Let Them Know You Love Them

The second principle involves openly and frequently letting your relatives or in-laws know that you care about them. All of us have different ways of expressing our love and concern for others. Perhaps you can learn from a more expressive and demonstrative partner, rather than question why they do what they do.

In my counseling office, I have had questions such as the following come up, each of which implies that what spouses are doing is not only different from the way they respond, it is also *wrong*.

"Why does he always have to call his parents every Sunday afternoon?"

"We never gave cards in our family for Easter and Mother's Day and Father's Day. Why is this so important?"

"She calls and asks her parents how she can pray for them for next week! Isn't that kind of odd?"

"When we go to visit, he always wants some time alone with each parent and each sibling. Why can't I be involved?"

All these acts are expressions of love and concern, and are normal. They help to alleviate one of the greatest fears we all face: the fear of abandonment. Not only do children struggle with this; adults also face it. When a child marries, parents wonder if they will still be a part of their child's life, and how much. Parents need reassurance. "Keeping in touch" is not a trite phrase, but a necessary ingredient for growing relationships. Building healthy relationships with parents and in-laws will help to nourish your own marriage relationship.

Taking Time to Build Relationships

Another principle is to develop the goal of building positive relationships with your in-laws. Three ingredients are necessary for any relationship to grow: time, attention and implementing biblical principles in the relationship.

You can choose whether or not to be involved with your relatives and in-laws. If you choose noninvolvement, you are essentially allowing others to control your life because you are allowing what they have done to influence you. If you choose involvement you are saying, "Regardless of who you are and what you have done, I am going to make every effort to build a relationship with you."

One mother-in-law said, "Our relationship started out kind of cool. Jean (my daughter-in-law) and I didn't seem to click. About a year after the wedding, she came by and asked to see my childhood pictures, and what I had saved. We had the best time sharing and laughing together. That broke the ice, and since then we've had a wonderful time.

"Before her baby was born, she asked my husband and me to write down 10 principles we had used in raising our son. That really created some talking between Frank (my husband) and me. But it was a wonderful time of reflection together. We even got out the picture album of Jim, and did a lot of reminiscing. And then Jean would share with me articles and books she was reading so I would know "where she was at" as she called it. We've all felt a part of one another and I'm so thankful she reached out to me."

I have heard of couples bringing both sets of parents together and sharing and comparing their family tree. It is amazing what you can learn through this experience.

A minister shared with me that on the last session of premarital counseling he asks both sets of parents to come along with the couple. Three significant subjects are addressed. Each set of parents is asked to share a prepared list of expectations they have for the couple after they are married. The couple has the opportunity to identify which expectations they can meet and which ones they cannot. Each father and mother talks about an ability or skill they have that they would be willing to share with the prospective son- or daughter-in-law if they so desire.

They also discuss the wedding day and the ceremony itself, to discover who wants what. Over the years, the cost of most of the weddings was reduced by 50 percent when everyone discovered that some of what they had planned was for the other party's benefit, but was not really desired.

Biblical Dynamics of Change

Building new and solid relationships requires change, and change can be frightening. Yet we can transform any relationship when we make a decision and a commitment to live our lives according to the Word of God. But to live and reflect something in our life, we not only have to *know* it; we have to give it time to seep into our lives and become part of our thought life and value system.

If someone tells you, "You're too old to change and to learn a new way of responding after all these years," that is *not true!*

If someone tells you it is easy to change if you set your mind to it, that, too, is *not true!*

Change is difficult, but possible. It takes energy, effort and time, but it is possible. The essence of our Christian faith is hope. In counseling situations, I have seen married couples change although I honestly did not believe it was possible!

We are creatures of habit; but the presence of Jesus Christ in our lives can override the habit patterns that have been constantly reinforced over the years.

Here are three proven steps. (1) Select a behavior you would like to change. (2) Decide how you would like to respond differently, and base it upon God's Word. (3) Memorize a related Scripture and repeat it 15 to 20 times a day.

Because our thought life is such a critical factor in how we respond to others and to ourselves, some of our relational habits may need radical reconstruction. Charles Swindoll describes it in this way:

> In order for old defeating thoughts to be invaded, conquered, and replaced by new, victorious ones, a process of reconstruction must transpire. The best place I know to begin this process of mental cleansing is with the all-important discipline of memorizing Scripture. I realize it doesn't sound very sophisticated or intellectual, but God's Book is full of powerful ammunition! And dislodging negative and demoralizing thoughts requires aggressive action. I sometimes refer to it as mental assault.[1]

Visualize yourself responding in the new way in several varied situations. Do this 15 to 20 times a day. If necessary, role-play the situation with a friend. Commit this new way of responding to God, and thank Him for what He will be doing in your life.

Measure your growth with new criteria. Instead of focusing on the 90 percent of the time you reverted back to the old pattern, dwell on the 10 percent when you came through.

Here are some Bible verses from *The New International Version* that are helpful in transforming family relationships:

A patient man has great understanding, but a quick-tempered man displays folly (Prov. 14:29).

A gentle answer turns away wrath, but a harsh word stirs up anger (Prov. 15:1).

A hot-tempered man stirs up dissension, but a patient man calms a quarrel (Prov. 15:18).

He who covers over an offense promotes love, but whoever repeats the matter separates close friends (Prov. 17:9).

A man's wisdom gives him patience; it is to his glory to overlook an offense (Prov. 19:11).

It is to a man's honor to avoid strife, but every fool is quick to quarrel (Prov. 20:3).

A word aptly spoken is like apples of gold in settings of silver (Prov. 25:11).

Rejoice with those who rejoice; mourn with those who mourn. Live in harmony with one another. Do not be proud, but be willing to associate with people of low position. Do not be conceited (Rom. 12:15,16).

Be completely humble and gentle; be patient, bearing with one another in love (Eph. 4:2).

Speaking the truth in love, we will in all things grow up into him who is the Head, that is, Christ (Eph. 4:15).

"In your anger, do not sin": Do not let the sun go down while you are still angry (Eph. 4:26).

Do not let any unwholesome talk come out of your mouths, but only what is helpful for building others up according to their needs, that it may benefit those who listen (Eph. 4:29).

Get rid of all bitterness, rage and anger, brawling and slander, along with every form of malice (Eph. 4:31).

Be kind and compassionate to one another, forgiving each other, just as in Christ God forgave you (Eph. 4:32).

Then make my joy complete by being like-minded, having the same love, being one in spirit and purpose. Do nothing out of selfish ambition or vain conceit, but in humility consider others better than yourselves. Each of you should look not only to your own interests, but also to the interests of others (Phil. 2:2-4).

Bear with each other and forgive whatever grievances you may have against one another. Forgive as the Lord forgave you (Col. 3:13).

Small Issues, Large Struggles

Another building block for good extended-family relationships involves learning to deal with disagreements and differences of opinion. Such conflicts are bound to arise with the merging of two families. It is amazing how often parents, in-laws and their children often end up in power struggles over small issues that become significant and last for years. No one learns to back off and discover a new approach. I am not sure the participants would agree to labeling their response a power struggle, but the evidence is there.

The word "power" means "the possession of control, authority or influence over others." *The Oxford English Dictionary* defines authority as "power or right to enforce obedience...the right to command or give an ultimate decision." Although a power struggle in a family does not mean anyone actually has this power, people often act as though they have it—and the difficulties often go unresolved.

We are dog lovers in our home. We enjoy them, and they have taught us much about life and people. Prior to the golden retriever we have now, we raised shelties. They look like miniature collies and are highly intelligent—until they get into a tug-of-war with another puppy. Then they both sit there and pull and pull on the object, neither of them getting anywhere.

But neither dog will give in. They wear themselves out pulling, and trying to get the object away from the other puppy. If they were to use the high level of intelligence with which they are gifted, they might come to the conclusion that what they are doing is not working. If one of them would let go of its hold on the object, the other would probably be knocked off balance, dislodging the object. Then the smart one could have the object all to himself.

I can remember sitting, watching and laughing as the struggle went on and on. Perhaps some of the laughter was at myself and others I know, for we are not much different from the puppies. Most people live with a fear of being dominated by others, so we dig in our heels and attempt to control others before they control us.

When a problem with parents or in-laws occurs, take the time to move from an emotional response to a thinking response. When you are able to do this, and to do it together, you will be able to consider options and alternatives.

Where to Go, What to Do?

One issue that often leads to a tug-of-war hinges on the question of where you spend the vacation, especially when your relatives or in-laws live in a different part of the country.

A 45-year-old husband told me, "When I was a kid I always went on vacation to places my parents wanted to go. I looked forward to getting married and then being able to take vacations where I wanted. That's a joke. Almost every year we end up visiting her folks and my folks. Visiting relatives isn't the same as a vacation!"

That is true for many people, unless everyone's needs and desires are considered. Regarding this issue, as well as many others, here are some options:

1. Going to parents and in-laws every other year.
2. Asking them to visit you more often.
3. Meeting at a recreational site such as a national park for the family get-together.
4. Splitting the vacation time between visiting and other activities.
5. Going alone to see one's own family part of the time while the other person is either working, traveling or doing something the other family members are not interested in doing.

One wife told me, "I go to my parents' for the first week of our vacation while my husband is backpacking with the boys. My idea of camping is staying at the Marriott for a weekend. When they come home then they join me at my parents'. I love the time alone with Mom and Dad, my husband and the boys have their fun, and when they arrive their attitude is great. This works out much better than what we used to do."

Do not be surprised if you receive criticism from your in-laws for making such arrangements. The important thing is how you respond to them. Too many times, the people being criticized are either intimidated or they overreact. Either kind of response simply perpetuates the problem.

Handling Criticism Creatively

Whether about vacations or many other issues, in-law relationships often involve criticism. Of the several possible ways of handling it, the following approach will work in most situations. But it *will not work* unless you (1) know the approach thoroughly; (2) put it into your own words; (3) practice what you will say several times until you are comfortable with the ideas; and (4) anticipate both positive and negative responses on the part of the people involved. This last point is essential in order not to be sidetracked from what you want to say. You may want to rehearse in advance with your spouse.

Listening to Your Critic

If someone criticizes you, stop what you are doing and look directly at the other person. By giving him or her your undivided attention, the irritation may be lessened.

Criticism seldom hits the bull's-eye, but it rarely misses the whole target.

Listen to what the person has to say. "He who answers a matter before he hears the facts, it is folly and shame to him" (Prov. 18:13). Try to hear what the person is *really* saying—what is behind the remarks. You may discover that you are merely the object of the other person's pent-up frustration, and that nothing personal is intended.

Accept the criticism as the other person's way of seeing things. From her perspective, her interpretation is accurate. And she could be right—so don't just write off the complaint. If she exaggerates, don't get hung up on attempting to correct her at this time.

If the person criticizing you asks why you did what you did, or why you do something a certain way, don't always feel you must give your reasons. Giving your reasons to others puts them at an advantage. They now know where they can attack you. You could say, "I just prefer doing it this way," or, "Well, I'm not sure my reasons are that crucial; tell me more about your concern," or, "Do you have a positive suggestion to offer? I would like to hear it so I can consider it and then make my choice."

Don't accuse your in-law of being oversensitive or irrational. That will only aggravate an already delicate situation.

Don't change the subject, or attempt to evade the present issue by joking about the complaint. It could be very important to your in-law.

Be open to the criticism and consider its possible validity before you respond. Criticism seldom hits the bull's-eye, but it rarely misses the whole target. This situation could be an opportunity for you to grow. You might thank the other person for bringing this to your attention, because it helps you know how that person is feeling.

Consider the following passages from Proverbs from *The Living Bible* about responding to criticism:

> If you refuse criticism you will end in poverty and disgrace; if you accept criticism you are on the road to fame (13:18).

> Don't refuse to accept criticism; get all the help you can (23:12).

> It is a badge of honor to accept valid criticism (25:12).

> A man who refuses to admit his mistakes can never be successful. But if he confesses and forsakes them, he gets another chance (28:13).

Responding to a Critic

If you can learn to respond to the facts of what your critic says, instead of reacting emotionally, you will find yourself in control of the situation. For example, consider this interaction:

Mother-in-law: "Mary, I see that the children are outside playing and they're not dressed warmly enough again." (She and Mary have had a running debate over this for several years. Mary could reply with any of the following.)

Mary: "Mother! They *are* dressed warmly enough. I've told you that before!"

Or: "Oh, I think they'll be OK. Don't you have something else to do?"

Or: "You feel that the children should have some more clothes on? Thank you for letting me know that. When it gets cold enough I'll see to it, or I might ask you to call them in for me."

Typical Criticisms

Following are three other typical statements an in-law might make when visiting your home. Remember, these could be just statements of fact, or they could be statements made simply for the purpose of getting a response from you. After each statement, write down how you would respond.

1. "I see you have your refrigerator full of leftovers again!"

2. "You mean our granddaughter went out on a date tonight? Didn't you tell her that we would be dropping by?"

3. "You don't call or write me as much as you used to."

In each case, your in-laws would probably expect you to give an explanation or to go on the defensive. But what would happen if you agreed with their statements? If you don't respond in the way that is expected, your in-laws may be forced to clarify what they really meant by the statement. Agreeing in principle with what someone has said does not mean that you change your own opinion or beliefs.

For example, what if Mary's conversation with her mother-in-law went something like this:

Mother-in-law: "Oh, I see you have your refrigerator full of left-overs again."

Mary: "Yes, I guess I do have some leftovers in there again."

Mother-in-law: "Well, some of them look like they have been in there for a long time."

Mary: "Yes, I am sure some of them have been in there too long."

Suggestions from in-laws may reflect some of their own needs, and may not really be attempts on their part to control or interfere.

You can see that this conversation could go on for some time without Mary's committing herself to any change. She has little chance, also, of offending her mother-in-law.

Consider this: What needs do your in-laws have at this time in their lives? Often the reason people behave in specific ways or resort to criticism is that they are seeking to fulfill particular needs of their own. Often their behavior does not accurately reflect what their needs are, so we are confused. Too often we react without considering why our critic is acting this way. Have you ever considered that the suggestions coming from your in-laws may reflect some of their own needs, and may not really be attempts on their part to control or interfere?

Inspection Time

Karen, a young woman attending a seminar, shared with me what had happened to her. Whenever her mother-in-law would come over to her home, she would constantly check the house for dust and dirt.

She was like a marine sergeant who wears a white glove to inspect the barracks.

One day, after Karen had worked for hours cleaning the house and scrubbing the floor, her mother-in-law came for a visit. As she sat in the kitchen, her eyes spotted a six-inch section of woodwork next to the tile that had been missed. As she mentioned this to her daughter-in-law, Karen could feel the anger slowly creeping up through her body. Her face started becoming tense and red.

For the first time, her mother-in-law noticed this reaction to her suggestions. She said to Karen, "Honey, I can't really be of much help to you in anything else, but this is one thing that I can help you with." As she shared, Karen realized that her mother-in-law felt inadequate and useless around her, and this was her only way of attempting to feel useful and needed. Now both women had a better understanding of one another.

Clarifying the Issues

Another important guideline in getting along with relatives is to clarify the relationship you want to have with them. I have seen so many family squabbles over the lack of clarification just on everyday issues such as privacy, visiting, phoning, lending or borrowing money, who does what for holidays and birthdays, and how to address each other.

A Gentle Confrontation

Ted, a man in his mid-30s, had lived with his mother until he was married four years earlier. He said he did this to save money, which makes sense. Sixteen months after the wedding, Ted and his wife, Faye, came into my office. Tension was developing between them over Ted's mother. Faye felt his mother was continually interfering in Ted's life.

Ted's mother phoned him or visited him often to contribute unsolicited advice. He tended to ignore what she said, except that he erupted with anger after she left. He refused to confront the problem head-on, but took it out on Faye as well as the people at work.

After listening to them tell their story, I asked Ted, "Is the way you are handling this problem with your mother working?"

"No, not really," he answered.

"Then you really don't have anything to lose by trying a different approach, do you?" I suggested.

"You're right," he agreed. "I've got nothing to lose and a lot to gain. I really love Faye and my mother, but I feel caught in the middle. I know Mom's intentions are good most of the time. Perhaps I've added to the problem by not moving away from home sooner, and maybe I've relied too much on her advice. Now I've got to handle this situation. I do wish she would back off but I haven't told her, have I?"

I offered a suggestion that has proved effective for most problems similar to Ted's. But it required that he adopt a new approach to the problem. He did not have to wait long to try out his new plan. The next week his mother called him at home and gave some suggestions for his vacation.

Ted listened to her patiently, then said, "Mom, I need to share something with you. I become a bit upset when you make so many suggestions on what Faye and I should do. I realize that you love us and want the best for us. And I love you, too. But now that I'm on my own and married, I need my independence. I enjoy some of our interaction, but too many suggestions bother me.

"I would like you to do something for me. I think it would work better if I called you once a week and you called me once a week. We can share what's going on in our lives. If you have a suggestion, please ask me first if I would like to hear your ideas on that subject. I think this way we will enjoy the relationship better."

Ted had prepared himself for several possible ways his mother might respond to this initial conversation. She could react with hurt. She did. She could become defensive and say she was just trying to be helpful. She did. She might withdraw by not calling for a week or two. She did. Or she could respond with statements of self-pity. She did.

In time, however, the relationship became much better. Ted had to repeat his request on two subsequent calls before it finally "took" with his mother. But it began to work.[2]

Clarifications Needed

Some people prefer to call their own parents "Mom" and "Dad," and would prefer not to use those terms for their in-laws. Clarify this by discussing it together.

Some people prefer to be called first, rather than having someone just drop in on them unannounced. Clarify this.

Some prefer not to be called during the dinner hour, but any other time is all right. Clarify this.

Some would prefer altering the location for family gatherings from time to time, rather than always going to the same home. Clarify this.

Will loans back and forth ever be made? If so, they need to be based clearly upon a business basis, including proper paperwork, payment schedule, interest rates and so on. It needs to be seen by all parties as a business transaction and be free of any hidden agendas.

What happens when your parents or in-laws become elderly or ill, and need additional care? What are your expectations for this? What are your spouse's, and what are the parents'? This is one of the unpleasant realities of life we will all face, and planning and discussing it in advance is extremely important.

Would you ever have your parents live with you, or would you provide for them financially, or will they be able to make it on their own?

What will you do when one of your parents dies? What will your role be? This, too, needs to be clarified.

Keeping It Together

Another guideline to follow is to respond as a united couple. Parents and in-laws need to understand that you and your partner are in agreement on issues. Don't let any relatives drive you apart.

Some couples have shared statements they have learned to use, such as, "We have discussed this and we have decided...." Using the word "we" carries a strong message. If a relative makes comments to you about your partner, don't cooperate with them by conveying this information back to your partner. Suggest that this is something they need to discuss directly with your spouse if they have this concern.

When you marry, your partner comes first. Unfortunately, far too many parents need to learn this. And they can, by your continued loyalty and support of your spouse.[3]

Reflecting on This Chapter

1. What have you done in the past to let both your own parents and your in-laws know they are important to you?

2. During the past two weeks, what have you done to express your positive feelings toward your parents and your in-laws?

3. What other things could you say or do that would let your parents and your in-laws know they are important to you?

4. What have you done to learn from your parents or in-laws the kind of relationship they expect from you and your spouse? (Such as how often to visit or call, their involvement in disciplining your children, etc.)

What should you do about this in the future?

5. In the past, how have you helped your parents or in-laws meet their own needs and develop greater meaning in life?

   How can you help them in the future?

6. If your parents or in-laws have had serious difficulties in the past, how did you respond to them?

   How can you be more helpful in the future?

7. In the past, what have you done with your parents or in-laws to make it easier for them to demonstrate love toward you and your immediate family?

   How can you improve this in the future?

8. What have you done in the past to assist your parents or in-laws to receive love from you?

9. What have you done to demonstrate your love to them?

Notes
   1. Charles Swindoll, *Living Above the Level of Mediocrity* (Dallas, TX: WORD Inc., 1987), p. 26.
   2. H. Norman Wright, *Family Is Still a Good Idea* (Ann Arbor, MI: Servant Publications, 1992), pp. 188-189, adapted.
   3. Miriam Arond and Samuel L. Parker, *The First Year of Marriage* (New York: Warner Books, 1987), pp. 49-53.

chapter
6

Making Peace with Your Mother-in-Law

LET ME LEAD YOU THROUGH SEVERAL DIFFERENT SCENARIOS, ONE OR MORE OF which may remind you of your relationship with your in-laws. But as you read them, remember that you will probably be a mother-in-law yourself. You may want to view these pictures through the eyes of the mother-in-law in you that is yet to be. Which portrayals contain scenes you would handle differently? Which scenes portray roles you could play some day?

Life with In-Laws

"She'll Never Take My Place"
It was the night before the wedding. The rehearsal had gone smooth-

ly, and the dinner would begin in a few minutes. But first, Jim's mother managed to take him by the arm and pull him aside. Putting her hands on his shoulders, she said:

"Jimmy, you're my son and you've turned out so well. I've given everything for you and it was worth every sacrifice. Please keep in mind that Tracy will never be able to do all the things that I have done for you. No woman could. Just remember your mother."

Later on, when the opportunity arose and no one else could hear, Jim's mother said to Tracy, "Dear, it's going to be difficult for you trying to live up to Jim's expectations of what a woman should do for him. Give it your best effort, and then when you need help, give me a call."

What a wedding gift! This one was designed to *create* strain, not lessen it. What do you think the first five years were like for this couple—and for the in-laws?

"You're Now Number One!"

Alan and Lauri were leaving the church following the reception when Alan's mother came rushing out with a formal looking piece of paper and a pen in her hand.

"I know you're eager to leave, and I want you to," she said, "but this is so important. It will take just a minute. Alan, I need your signature on this form. I've already signed it."

Alan looked puzzled but took the paper, quickly read it and then with a big smile signed it with a flourish and handed it back to his mother.

His mother then gave the form to Lauri, and with moist eyes and a friendly smile said, "Lauri, this paper belongs to you—and so does Alan. I used to be the Number One woman in Alan's life. I will always be his mother, but this is my declaration that I'm transferring the position of being Number One woman to you.

"This is a signed certificate giving this position to you, as well as my announcement to Alan, to be sure that he understands this change. Have a wonderful honeymoon. I love you both."

With that, Alan's mother turned and walked away with both Lauri and Alan smiling; but now the tears were in their eyes.

This, too, was a wedding gift; but this one was positive. What do you think the first five years were like for this couple?

"We Can Hardly Wait!"

Henry came from a large family. He was the last born, as well as the only son. Two weeks prior to the wedding his mother had dropped in to see his fiancée, Kathy, at her work. She had timed her coffee break so the two of them could step outside and talk. Henry's mother came right to the point.

"Kathy, I've had a couple of concerns about Henry's marrying you. You seem kind of frail, and I worry about your health at times. It's so important in our family line, and you know that Henry is our only son.

"I'm sure you want several children, and I know Henry wants a son. Heaven knows we can hardly wait for the grandchild you're going to present us with. So I just wanted you to know that I'll be sending you a Mother's Day card each year to encourage you not to wait too long to have children. If the two of you should have any difficulty having children, I just want you to know that the problem is not on our side of the family. It would have to be on yours."

Can you imagine how this made Kathy feel about herself, her mother-in-law and her future marriage? Perhaps we don't even want to imagine what the first five years of marriage were going to be like.

"Welcome to the Family!"

In premarital counseling sessions, I ask the future parents-in-law to write a letter to their prospective son- or daughter-in-law, stating why they are looking forward to that person becoming their son- or daughter-in-law. This is shared with the person at the final counseling session. I ask them to read it aloud. The following is a letter from the groom's mother to her future daughter-in-law:

Dearest Dara,

Well, this is a Red Letter Day.

A little over three years ago you came into our lives. Now it looks like we get to officially claim you for our very own daughter. PTL!

The fact that Steve has chosen you to become his bride means that you are an answer to prayer.

In receiving you as a daughter we must be willing to give up our claim on "he's all ours" concerning Steve.

Among the outstanding qualities I have noticed in you is your willingness to share your time with Steve, with me and with Dad. Thank you for your *un*selfishness.

This quality goes hand in hand many times with self-sacrifice, which is a very important aspect of expressing one's love for others as far as I am concerned.

Yes, I have noticed your efforts and encouragement toward Steve to have some quality time with us as well as with you alone. This encourages me that you will not let us be forgotten after you become husband and wife.

Your willingness to serve the Lord as part of a team effort as well as an individual is something I admire in you.

Although you become one upon marriage, you will still be accountable to the Lord as an individual.

Your personal relationship with the Lord will make a big difference in what kind of wife you will make for our son. Keep up the good work, honey.

I see prayer as an important part of your life. This is a *very* important part of marriage these days. With Steve in full-time service, he will be subject to more temptations and trials than the average husband would be. Bathe him daily in much prayer! Remember 1 Thessalonians 5:17 and Philippians 4:6,7.

Do not forget to pray for yourself! Remember you are *one* in this marriage and ministry.

You will have need of physical, spiritual and emotional strength at times that you think you can not go a step further.

The same goes for Steve. Pray for wisdom in the little things as well as the big things. The little foxes spoil the grapes. Little things often get to our weak undersides quicker than the big trials.

God has given you a creative mind, and the ability to put ideas into action. This will be a real asset in your marriage if you seek wisdom in how to use it physically, spiritually, sexually and emotionally. *Go for it!*

You're a sensitive and tenderhearted person. This makes me happy because I have a soul mate to cry with over special times and stories. Just a little bonding factor! God often uses this gift to help us be sensitive both to spiritual and physical needs in others. You may take teasing over your tears, but let God use that heart in your marriage at times when no words have been shared concerning a need.

Being teachable is already paying off in more ways than you know. Part of which has endeared you to my heart, even before this pre-engagement time.

It has been encouraging watching you grow in many ways these last three years.

I want you to know that I will continue praying for you and supporting you with love as you become part of our family.

With love,
Mom Brown

With a welcome like that, a marriage relationship, as well as family relationships, have the potential for flourishing that they need.

Cutting the Apron Strings
A father described a choice experience that graphically communicated the transfer of alliance:

I'll never forget the wedding of one of my best college friends, John Engstrom, years ago. Actually it wasn't the wedding itself that impressed me as much as something that happened at the rehearsal dinner. Mrs. Engstrom, John's mom, was seated at the front table with John, his bride, and the bride's parents. At a particular time at the dinner, Mrs. Engstrom stood up and pulled out a beautifully wrapped box. She unwrapped it, and with great ceremony displayed one of her favorite old aprons. Holding the apron high for everyone to see, she reached into her purse and brought out a big pair of scissors. With a flourish, she snipped off the apron strings and handed them to John's bride-to-be.

"Never again," she said, "will I have the same place in John Engstrom's life. You are now the woman in his life."

It was a moment of formal releasing, in front of many witnesses. And the most significant witnesses of all were a young bride and groom. It was a profound moment... but a joyful one, too. There was a feeling of rightness (and rite-ness) about it all.[1]

Five different scenarios, two negative and three positive, with some fairly predictable results.

Predictable Problems from the New Mom

A mother is like the lead-off runner in a relay race. In time, she hands the baton of leadership to her husband, and they work together in raising their son. Then, a new woman comes into the picture—one who takes the central role with their son. They all have the potential for closeness, harmony, love and respect—or for conflict, power struggles and constant tension.

Is it possible to know in advance that major problems loom on the horizon? Yes, there are signs to read and warnings to take to heart.

A mother is like the lead-off runner in a relay race. In time, she hands the baton of leadership to her husband, and they work together in raising their son.

The "Perfect" Son

If a mother feels her son can do no wrong, and lets the daughter-in-law know this, trouble is brewing. Mother is living in denial—a dreamworld. She probably believes that her son is perfect because any admission that he is imperfect would be a negative reflection on her parenting.

Sometimes frustrations in a mother's own marriage cause her to seek some sort of fulfillment through her son's marriage. And when her son doesn't perform according to Mother's expectations, imagine who will be responsible! The daughter-in-law is living under the eye of the judge.

"Here's a List…"

Another predictable problem occurs when a mother-in-law either tells her daughter-in-law or hands her a list of what she would like her to do to motivate her son to make his mother happy. I have seen the pressure this can put upon the young wife.

One daughter promptly gave the list back to her mother-in-law and said, "Since you've tried all these years and have so much more ability than I, it's a foregone conclusion that I won't be able to motivate Jim to do these things. But why don't *you* give him this list? Now that he's married, perhaps he'll respond better."

The Invading Mother-in-Law

Another sure sign of a problem is when a mother-in-law is critical of her daughter-in-law's background, where they choose to live, her decision to work or not to work and her choice of occupation. This type of intrusiveness and criticism is really a violation of the integrity of the daughter-in-law, and this attitude shows no respect. Often this criticism expands throughout the years. It may appear especially in the realm of child rearing.

Mothers-in-law who are invaders tend to use the words "should" and "ought" excessively as they impose their standards on others. "Should" and "ought" imply, "I know better than you do and you ought to listen to me."

This problem has a fairly predictable outcome; it is called, "Shut out mother-in-law." Conversations become abstract, and detailed plans are omitted from conversations. Avoidance is the order of the day, and this leads to greater deterioration of the relationship. Criticism and advice are more likely to be heard when "maybe" is substituted for "ought" and "should."

One young (and courageous) wife, after hearing several "shoulds" and "oughts," shared with her mother-in-law the following statement:

"Joan, there are times when what you say makes sense, but for me the packaging of what you say could change just a bit and I would receive it better. Perhaps you could begin substituting the word 'maybe' for 'should' and 'ought.' And while you're learning, whenever you forget and use the old words I will simply remind you by saying the word, 'maybe.' Perhaps that will help." This is a positive way to handle a delicate situation.

Another way of responding would be to reflect back what was said and to ask for clarification. For example, Marsha's mother-in-law says, "You shouldn't let the children run around outside without a jacket on!" Marsha's response is, "You don't want them outside without their jackets. You seem to be concerned about them. Could you tell me what your concern is, Mother?"

This shows she is listening, is not defensive and takes control of the direction of the conversation.

A third approach is to agree in principle with what the other has said, but both parties realizing this doesn't mean you have changed your own opinion or stance.

Mother-in-law: "I see you're letting Jimmy play with that neighbor boy again."

Judy: "Yes, they're playing in our neighbors' backyard."

Mother-in-law: "Well, that little boy looks like something the dogs have dragged in."

Judy: "His play clothes do look like they've seen better days, don't they?"

As was the case in the previous conversation regarding leftovers in the refrigerator, this exchange could go on and on without Judy's committing herself to any change, but also with little possibility of offending her mother-in-law.

In healthy in-law relationships in which there is a high level of involvement and intimacy, suggestions and comments like these can be made without causing a problem.

The Surrogate Daughter

Another indicator of potential difficulty is the mother-in-law's desire for her daughter-in-law to fill that empty space in her life that results from not having her own daughter. This is a message loaded with expectations that probably cannot be met.

It also reflects possessiveness. I have talked with wives who said their mother-in-law told them before the wedding how delighted they were to be gaining a daughter, but they never seemed satisfied with what their daughter-in-law gave. The daughter-in-law was expected to respond to her mother-in-law just like a daughter who had bonded with her all of her life.

One wise young wife told me that when her mother-in-law kept referring to her as her daughter, she said, "Millie, I can never be your daughter or fulfill your expectations of what a daughter should be. But I can be your daughter-in-law, with all of it's limitations, and I'll work at being a good one."

Obstacles Raised by the New Wife

But it is not just mothers-in-law who instigate difficulties. Many mothers-in-law respond to their son's marriage in a loving, healthy way, only to find the daughter-in-law raising potential problems. Just as all the issues that stem from the mother-in-law are not covered here, so it is with issues a daughter-in-law creates. But these are some of the most common ones.

The Rescuer Bride

A common problem I have seen for years is the situation in which the young husband either altogether forgets his mother's birthday, anniversary or Valentine's Day, or remembers such occasions only once in awhile. Too often the wife jumps in and takes over the responsibility, either of her own initiative or through some indirect hints on the part of his mother. Then if she backs off on doing his job for him, in the hope that he has learned to handle it himself, she will receive the blame because mother has known all along who has been the instigator.

The best way to handle this problem is for the couple and his mother to sit down and have his mother share with her son what she wants from him and why. His wife can let both her mother-in-law and her husband know that she will not be responsible for reminding him of his responsibilities.

Expectations Based on Mom

Some daughters-in-law find themselves basing their relationship with a mother-in-law on a poor relationship with their own mother. When this happens, they often end up responding to their new mother-in-law in one of two different ways. If they expect their mother-in-law to fill the empty places in their lives left by their own mom, they can become too needy, pushy, controlling or disappointed. The young woman may be disappointed when her mother-in-law declines to become wrapped up in her life. Then she may take out her feelings on her husband.

On the other hand, a bride may distance herself from her new mother-in-law if she feels that because she has tried once with one mother she isn't about to risk the hurt again. So the mother-in-law never really has much of a chance to begin with.

Low Self-Esteem

If the daughter-in-law struggles with intense personal insecurities or an inadequate sense of self-esteem, she may be afraid of interacting with her mother-in-law. She may go along with whatever the older woman suggests, and resent it later. A daughter-in-law who has low self-esteem will tend to downgrade her own wants and desires to please others, but this doesn't build her self-esteem. It actually lessens it, because she ends up losing.

A woman who has low self-esteem may become possessive about her husband. Why? Because she feels inadequate and insecure about her ability to hold him. Perhaps she married out of the need to have someone help her feel good about herself, failing to realize that you can't be happily married to another person unless you're happily married to yourself.

Living with the potential fear of losing her husband can cast others in the role of a threat. This includes friends, coworkers as well as her husband's mother. She may also work at isolating her husband from his mother.

Rigidity and the Need to Control

Another issue is best illustrated by what a new daughter-in-law gave to her mother-in-law. It was called "Newlywed Rules for In-laws to

Follow." You can't believe what was on that list. It was difficult to take it seriously, but the young wife was dead serious. The list specified:

1. The days of the month they could visit.
2. The times of the month they could visit.
3. The frequency of visits during the month.
4. At least twelve hours' notice if they wanted to stop over or drop something off.
5. How often they could call.
6. How much they would be able to spend on gifts for them.
7. And from now on, they would spend Christmas with her parents and Thanksgiving with them.

Such rules that reflect the need to control and a high degree of inflexibility are sure ways to offend, alienate and block the development of a relationship. All the subjects mentioned above are good to discuss, but no one is helped by having rules dictated to them! If a daughter-in-law is this rigid and controlling, it's going to be very stressful for the man caught in the middle.

One of the most painful scenarios for parents-in-law is when their married son is held hostage...by his wife.

Holding Hubby Hostage
Perhaps one of the most painful scenarios for parents-in-law is when their married son is held hostage...by his wife. I have not only talked to husbands who have to clear *everything* with their wife, in one case people would have to clear an engagement or activity *with* him through her! Believe it or not.

I have talked with mothers-in-law who told me they literally lost their son when he married. Eventually they felt abandoned. One woman said her daughter-in-law came to one activity at her house, but two years later she had not been back. At first, her son Jim continued to come by himself, but lately he hasn't been coming, either. Two of his friends have called her asking what is going on, because it appears Jim isn't being allowed to see them. Someone is trying to isolate Jim, and in time he will likely leave!

A Process of Refinement

I would guess that all marriages and in-law relationships go through struggles as part of the normal refinement process. When two families are brought together by a marriage, more potential exists for hurt and discord because of family history, loyalty, dysfunction and ability to accept change and someone new.

I also suspect that more mother/daughter-in-law relationships are positive than negative. The people involved simply go on their way, relating through life, not saying much. It is the problem cases that are more obvious.

Another way to look at these relationships is to realize that the Christian faith and lifestyle can certainly override and replace the problem patterns. But we usually leave this as a last resort. Praying for one another, praying with one another if possible, looking at specific Bible passages to discover how to apply them to the relationship and giving one another the benefit of the doubt can be important keys.

One couple met with both sets of parents, had everyone make a list of their own strengths and weaknesses, and then shared them with one another. All of them had taken the Myers-Briggs Type Indicator, a well-known personality inventory, and they spent more than one session together discovering one another's uniqueness and how best to relate to each other.

Just as a married couple has to discover their differences and learn to make adjustments, so does an in-law relationship. Two firstborns who marry must learn to accept and adjust. It is no different when the mother-in-law and daughter-in-law are firstborns. They can easily clash if they don't have a high degree of acceptance and understanding.

A couple in which one is an extrovert and the other an introvert can have a rich and wonderful relationship if they learn the unique characteristics of the other and learn to adapt their responses in order to honor and respect these unique features. If they don't, they will push their partner away and soon have a distanced relationship. It will be the same in any in-law relationship as well.

I have seen extroverted daughters-in-law overwhelm their mothers-in-law, as well as the other way around. Can you imagine the stress experienced by an introvert wife as she goes on vacation with her husband and his extroverted parents and siblings for a week? I can, because I've seen it. I wish every adult family member would read the book *Type Talk* by Otto Kroeger and Janet Thuesen (Delacorte Press, 1988), and apply the content. I have seen scores of families who have done just this, and the results are amazing.

General Guidelines

People on every side of the in-law question ask for guidelines for relating to each other. The following have been gleaned from many sources through the years.

1. Don't complain to your spouse about the person to whom you have trouble relating. It won't help for you to complain about your mother-in-law to your husband, her son. Sons have said, "I wish my wife wouldn't complain to me about Mom, and how bad she is. I know she can get overly involved at times, but she's my mother and I don't really like anyone bad-mouthing her."

Neither will it help if the mother-in-law complains to her son about his wife, or to her husband about their daughter-in-law. I have heard fathers-in-law say, "I wish she wouldn't try to enlist my support for her cause. I don't feel the way she does and besides...I get along all right with my daughter-in-law."

2. Be sure to include your in-laws in significant family events. Even if the others live so far away they could never attend, they would appreciate being thought of. Purposeful exclusion because of problems and hurts serves only to deepen the distance between everyone.

3. Give the grandparents plenty of time with their grandchildren. Remember that they can enjoy and learn from one another. If the parents have a concern over different styles of discipline, safety features, health factors, differences in lifestyles and philosophies of living, these should be discussed together—including the most awkward and painful.

I heard of a family in which the father-in-law had sexually abused his own daughters. It had never been reported, and the mother-in-law was not aware of it. When this young couple had a daughter, the two sisters-in-law told them about what had happened, and expressed their concern. For years this couple worked on making sure their daughter was never left alone nor stayed overnight with the in-laws. The mother-in-law could never understand, and the relationship became very strained. I don't know if the issue was ever resolved.

4. Don't interfere in disagreements. I have seen both the parents-in-law as well as the younger couple appeal to the other to take their side in an argument. It doesn't work. Keep your conflicts and resolution in your own family. Avoid triangular patterns; for example, going through one person to communicate with the other.

5. Respect each other's privacy, and the amount of time the other family would like to spend alone. Don't invite yourself to outings and get-togethers. And if you weren't invited, don't pry or make comments about it. Assume that the event didn't involve you, that there was a legitimate reason not to invite you, or that it was an unintentional oversight. Give everyone the benefit of the doubt.

6. When your in-laws do something that is really upsetting, discuss it with them. Reinforce all the behaviors that you appreciate, and don't dwell on those that are different or that you don't understand.

All of you are joining a foreign culture in a sense. Just as people in a blended family who have children from different marriages may take five to six years to adjust to each other, count on in-law relationships taking at least that long. Give the relationship time to grow.

7. *If you find some interests in common, enjoy them.* If not, accept the fact without trying to force the other to like what you like. Do not feel obligated to engage in activities you could not care less about. Don't compare any other in-law style with your own.

8. *Don't blame any in-law for a problem that you may have in your own marriage.* And don't blame them when your spouse isn't as supportive of you as you would wish. It will only spread your difficulties to others.

9. *Be sensitive about informational boundaries.* Some questions just don't need to be asked. Don't get into how much each other earns, what you pay for major (and even minor) items, how much interest you're paying, what you give to the church and so on, unless both parties are comfortable with the discussion and agree that it won't affect the relationship. Before asking a question on a sensitive topic, ask yourself, "Is this going to benefit the relationship? Is it something I need to know?"[2]

10. *Anticipate that your relationship will grow and continually improve.* One of the best ways for this to happen is to ask how you can pray for each other, and to let the other know you are doing just that. Jeremiah 29:11 is applicable for in-law relationships as well as other ventures in life: "For I know the thoughts and plans that I have for you, says the Lord, thoughts and plans for welfare and peace, and not for evil, to give you hope in your final outcome."

Binding and Casual Relationships

Are your in-law relationships casual or binding? What do I mean by this?

Binding relationships are those that have more permanency, depth and commitment to one another. You may have a binding relationship not only with your spouse, but with parents, children, friends—even your employee or employer.

Everyone also has some casual involvements with others. Each time we see them it's fairly predictable what will be said. Our conversation is usually at the superficial or cliché level. Casual relationships are those we have with acquaintances, distant friends, neighbors down the street or anyone we relate to apart from a permanent or long-term relationship.

Some in-law relationships fit into this category. You know the ones I mean. They are the kind in which you see each other once or twice a year.

It's not uncommon to be in a binding relationship that is being treated as a casual relationship by one or both parties. Some of these are by mutual consent. Others exist because of tension and discord, or the desire of one party to keep it casual.

We have all inherited relationships either by bloodlines or through marriage in which we truly wish we'd been left out of the will! Do you have any casual relationships in your life that you wish you didn't have? Do you have any binding relationships in your life that you wish you didn't have? If so, you should realize that this isn't uncommon. We just don't click with some people, and we would never spend time with them save for the fact there is some family connection. Yet such relationships don't have to be a burden, nor a cause for stress and tension.

The quality and intensity of these connections will vary depending on several factors such as time, distance, frequency of contact, the parent-child relationship, personality similarities and differences, hindering dysfunctions in a person or the family unit and so on.

Most people, however, hunger for positive relationships built upon emotional closeness or intimacy. Marriage, of course, carries with it this promise; and it should not surprise us if such expectations extend to some extent to the in-law connection as well. In a sense, marriage unites two families as well as two people. The relationship is therefore usually expected to be binding rather than casual.

Polite Toleration

But some in-laws turn out to be unapproachable. If any kind of rejection or wounding words occur, you can count on several destructive patterns developing. At worst, defensiveness rears its head. Striking back may occur, listening goes by the wayside and assertions tend to turn into aggressions.

At best, the relationship exists at a level that is nothing more than what I call the Polite Toleration Relationship (PTR). It's basically the least involved relationship a person can have. In such a relationship, the people want to be able to converse with one another on a merely casual, everyday level, having no anger or discomfort.

The couples themselves may become polarized. The wife, for example, may be involved firsthand in the conflict, and her husband not only hears it secondhand but is torn by loyalty to both women in his life. I have heard both mothers-in-law and daughters-in-law make the same statement to rationalize the reason for distance in their relationship: "Oh, we just have nothing in common." Unfortunately, this can continue for decades—shallow, polite relationships based upon outward toleration of each other, which thinly covers the unexpressed pain and yearning of, "I wish it could be different."

Family members at this level don't usually share help, emotional support or love with each other. Their involvement is basically only what is necessary to meet the requirements of coexistence.

The Moderate Relationship

The next step up is considered a moderate relationship. Now we add the important dimension of emotional support. You and your in-laws are connected by some emotional give and take. A degree of openness enables both of you to share and hear each other's hurts, concerns, joys and needs.

Matt, a man in his mid-20s, told me, "Norm, when Tess and I married, I was so happy that she and Mom hit if off so well. They're able to care, cry and pray together, and Mom has too much respect for Tess to meddle in our lives."

Many mothers- and daughters-in-law have this quality relationship, many others do not but would like to have it.

The Quality Relationship

A final level of relational involvement is called the quality relationship. What does this mean? This is a relationship in which you can minister to one another in meaningful and tangible ways. Some people minister to others, but without emotional investment. The relationship is therefore shallow. But a quality relationship goes deep; there is mutual trust. When you share with another person at this level you feel safe enough to share your needs, thoughts and feelings. You can disagree with one another without affecting the quality of the relationship.[3]

Levels of Communication

The quality of your relationships is usually reflected in the level of your communication. Let's consider this as you reflect upon your in-law relationships.

Relationships generally have five levels of communication. In the exercises at the end of this chapter you will have the opportunity to evaluate each level as it relates to your relationship with your in-laws.

Level 1—Sharing Information

The first level of conversation is limited to sharing facts, explanations or information. Conversations at this level are much like exchanging newspaper stories. Although the information can be interesting, it is often considered small talk, and it really does not accomplish much in the way of getting to know another person. The degree of intimacy at this conversation level is extremely shallow.

Level 2—Speaking of Others
The second level of conversation centers on either talking about other people, or sharing the ideas and opinions of others. Conversation at this level is a bit more interesting, and yet discloses very little of one-self. Practically no intimacy is achieved when discussion is limited to persons outside the relationship, or to others' ideas instead of each other's.

Level 3—Minor Vulnerability
Conversation level three produces moderate intimacy. At this level you are sharing your own ideas and opinions. You are disclosing some of your own thoughts, and risking minor vulnerability. But you are still not revealing who you really are.

Level 4—Sharing More Personally
This level involves a higher degree of intimacy in conversation. Now you are sharing personal preferences, beliefs, concerns and some of your own personal experiences.

One of the level four questions my daughter often asked me when she was young was, "Daddy, what were you like when you were a little boy?" I was amazed at how much I would begin to recall and share about myself in response to her question.

Level 5—Sharing Your Inner Self
At the highest—or deepest—level of conversation and communication, you share your inner feelings and preferences, your likes and dislikes. You share what is occurring within your inner life, and you open up completely. You move beyond talking about events or beliefs or ideas or opinions. You talk about how these ideas or events or people influence you, and how they touch you emotionally and inwardly. At this level, emotional expression has moved from talking from the head to talking from the heart.[4]

Being of the Same Mind

One last suggestion remains. Actually, it's not a suggestion, but a directive written by the apostle Paul as directed by God. Think what could happen if these words guided our relationships!

> Fill up and complete my joy by living in harmony and being of the same mind and one in purpose, having the same love, being in full accord and of one harmonious mind and intention. Do nothing from factional motives—through contentiousness, strife, selfishness or for unworthy ends—or prompted by conceit and empty arrogance. Instead, in the true spirit of humility (lowliness of mind) let each regard the others as better than and superior to himself—thinking more highly of one another than you do of yourselves. Let each of you esteem and look upon and be concerned for not [merely] his own interests, but also each for the interests of others. Let this same attitude and purpose and [humble] mind be in you which was in Christ Jesus.—Let Him be your example in humility (Phil. 2:2-5).

> Be gentle and forbearing with one another and, if one has a difference (a grievance or complaint) against another, readily pardoning each other; even as the Lord has freely forgiven you, so must you also [forgive] (Col. 3:13).

> And whatever you do—no matter what it is—in word or deed, do everything in the name of the Lord Jesus and in [dependence upon] His Person, giving praise to God the Father through Him (Col. 3:17).

Reflecting on This Chapter

1. What are the binding relationships in your life?

2. What are the casual relationships in your life?

3. What are the binding relationships in your life that have a casual quality?

4. What relationships in your life would you like to have more binding?

5. What family members in your life fit into the category of "polite toleration"? How do you feel about them? What kind of relationship would you like with them?

6. With what family members do you have a "moderate" level relationship? How do you feel about them and what kind of relationship would you like with them?

7. Who are the family members in your life with whom you have a "quality" relationship? How do you feel about them? Do you enjoy this level of relationship with them?

8. On what kinds of occasions does a first-level, information-only level of communication tend to occur in your in-law relationships?

   a. Which of you tends to use this style of conversation most?
   b. What percentage of your conversation tends to occur at this level? (Circle one)
     10% 20% 30% 40% 50% 60% 70% 80% 90%

9. With which of your in-laws do you usually converse about others, or about the ideas of others?

10. With which of your in-laws do you share "minor vulnerability"?

11. With which of your in-laws do you share personal thoughts, beliefs and preferences?

12. With which of your in-laws are you totally open, and willing to share your inner self?

   What percentage of your conversation with these people occurs at this level? (Circle one)
   10%   20%   30%   40%   50%   60%   70%   80%   90%

Notes
1. Stu Weber, *Tender Warrior* (Sisters, OR: Questar, 1993), pp. 165-166.
2. Penny Bilofsky and Fredda Sacharow, *In-laws, Out-laws* (New York: Villard Books, 1991), pp. 235-243.
3. Carol C. Flax and Earl Ubell, *Mother, Father, You* (Ridgefield, CT: Wyden Books, 1980), pp. 192-201.
4. H. Norman Wright, *Holding on to Romance* (Ventura, CA: Regal Books, 1992), p. 165.

Part III

Understanding Your Own Son

chapter
7

Sons: To Have, to Hold and to Let Go

IT WAS A TYPICAL SCENE IN A SHOPPING MALL. HUNDREDS OF MOTHERS WITH what seemed to be thousands of kids were walking, talking and shopping. Some mothers were delighted to be there, others seemed satisfied, but many them looked as though they were ready to kill.

The interaction between some of the mothers and their sons was varied, too. I noticed some of them hanging on to their child with a viselike grip. The son was just following along compliantly. Other mothers and sons were engaged in a massive power struggle. I saw one mother literally dragging her resistant child along. His heels were dug into the floor, and he was screaming over and over again, "Let me go! Let me go!"

Other mothers were giving their sons explicit instructions about where to go, what to do, how to act and when to be back. I did see one mother ask her boy what he wanted to do and when he wanted to be picked up. He told her, and she took off to do her thing while he went his way, free as a bird.

Hanging On, Letting Go

Although most of this book deals with in-law relationships as they involve your husband, this chapter deals with how to raise your own sons to be healthy, secure men and husbands.

I'm sure you've seen scenarios such as those just described. Perhaps you've experienced them yourself. But let's change the picture a bit. Keep the mother's responses the same, but let's alter the ages of the sons a bit. Instead of a young boy, let's change them all to 25-year-old adults.

Have you ever seen a mother hanging on to that adult son with a viselike grip? I have.

Have you ever seen a mother trying to drag her adult son along, while he resists and yells, "Let go of me! Will you ever let go of me!"? I have.

Have you ever seen a mother dictating every move for her adult son, including what to do, when, how and for how long? I have.

I have also seen many mothers who have relinquished their sons. They progressively let go as their sons grew through childhood and adolescence, so that eventually they were properly launched.

It is not always an easy process. Perhaps we assume that it is common for it to be just an everyday, easy transition. Not so.

"Please Release Me, Let Me Go!"

In his book *Parenting Isn't for Cowards*, Dr. Jim Dobson describes a survey he conducted with a group of adult children. He asked for the top concerns they had in relating to their parents. It was interesting to note that the concerns included in-laws, aging, the spiritual condition of non-Christian parents, grandparents who weren't interested in their grandchildren and—the number one concern—the inability or unwillingness of parents to release their adult children.[1]

You don't suddenly just let go of a child. It takes years of education and preparation. It's a gradual building process for both your son and for you, involving growth and great flexibility, which, unfortunately, seem to be more and more difficult the older we become.

The older we grow as parents, the more ingrained our mind-set becomes. A mind-set is how we think. It's our settled opinion, based upon our years of experience, beliefs, knowledge and background. It could be very balanced and healthy, but totally divergent from our son's mind-set. Our mind-set could also be off base and inaccurate in many ways. But whether it's healthy or unhealthy, it will affect your relationship with your son.[2]

The authors of *When Your Kids Aren't Kids Anymore* write:

> Like cholesterol that builds up in the human arteries, some of these "settled opinions" need to be broken up and stirred to permit new thinking to occur. Yet we have found that our old ideas, our prejudices, and the pride of our past decisions and experiences are so very hard to overcome.[3]

Essential Transitions

To continue a healthy adult-to-adult relationship with an adult child, several transitions must occur.

From Teacher to Learner

One necessary transition is to move from being your son's teacher to being able to learn from him. As he grows older, your son will introduce you to new facets of the world. Some you will like, and some you won't; some will be comfortable and some won't. But to continue a relationship with any adult child, your view of the world will have to be expanded.

It is difficult for most of us as parents to admit that what we believe or the way we evaluate life is faulty or a bit off-center. We resist being "shown up," or discovering we've been wrong all these years—especially by a young offspring. Yet it's a sign of deepening

Cutting the cord between mother and son is a process that has to be relived from time to time.

maturity on our part to make this admission. It is essential in building a healthy adult-to-adult relationship.

Admitting mistakes of the past and present indicates to our adult child that we're open and ready to change.[4]

The initial step of relinquishment for a mother comes in the transfer of the baton to the father, as we discussed in chapter 1. If this is accomplished successfully (and the father cooperates by assuming his role), the relinquishment to adulthood will be an easier transition. You were probably thinking of your husband and his own upbringing as you read chapter 1. And relinquishment can certainly be a problem for a grown man, even if his mother lives far away. Now, however, I want you to reflect on how your own children will make the transition from your home to theirs.

One mother was praying for her son, who was 12 years old, when she imagined herself holding a large pair of scissors. She said she asked Jesus to hold her hands and help her to cut the cord between herself and her son. She said He did, and her son has been free to move toward manhood.

This mother also stated, however, that this is a process that has to be relived from time to time. When her children get upset with her, it's usually because she crossed over the line and pulled the cord again.

As a mother, one of the steps you will need to take with your son is to let him be who he is. Otherwise he may forcibly break away in order to become himself. He needs validation and affirmation for who he is. Putting a roadblock in his way may cause him to distance himself for years.

The relationship between any parent and child will be both a growing experience and a challenge. When a son is young, you are the authority and the person in control. But each year of your life you gradually give up a bit of the control and transfer some of it to your son. You're starting the process of working yourself out of a job. Self-sufficiency for your son is the goal.

Controller, Coach and Counselor
Your young son, or daughter, should know as a young child that you are in control. Gradually, however, the role of controller will begin to give way to a parenting style that is more along the lines of a coach. Even then, your coaching has a certain ring of authority. The task for your son is to follow your guidance, teaching and correction.

Eventually you begin to move toward the next role of parenting, that of a counselor. The time will come when your son will make his own decisions and decide on the direction of his life for himself, but early in this stage he needs to draw on you for guidance and counsel. Remember to let him *ask* for your counsel, rather than imposing it on him. During transitional stages, you may find yourself being controller, counselor and coach all at the same time, but in different arenas.

From Counseling to Mutuality
The adult-to-adult stage involves a blending of mutual counsel and mutual caring. The best word to describe your goal at this stage is "mutuality."[5]

How does a mother accomplish this task? Hopefully, she won't have to do it alone, but in partnership with her husband. The transition is much smoother when two parent-partners can work together, having mutual goals and styles. In an earlier book, I described the various styles of parenting that are so vital.[6]

Parents as Explorers

In a sense, healthy parents are really explorers. In order to properly teach, guide, encourage and nurture your child, you must patiently observe and study him to discover his unique personality traits and learning characteristics. The better you know your child, the more satisfying this mutual relationship will be for everyone concerned, and the better equipped he will be for a meaningful life.

An explorer mother and father are in a good position to implement the maturity and independence of their children. They develop the skill of asking questions. This is especially useful in the empowering techniques of teaching, participating and delegating. It is important that your questions be nonthreatening, in order for them to be a creative tool for helping a child think about and identify his options for independence.

Parents as Gardeners

A gardener considers each plant unique. A gardener doesn't force a potato to be an apple. Similarly, parents interested in providing the right kind of cultivation for their children recognize the uniqueness of each child. They nurture that tender plant to full maturity and fruitfulness. Accepting his or her personality, they adapt their responses to it.

One man shared this with me: "Fortunately, I came out of a home where I was accepted for who I was at all times. I was accepted when I blew it, as well as when I achieved. I knew I was loved at all times. That was probably the best gift my parents ever gave to me. And I want to be able to do this with the people in my life as well."

During the 1992 Winter Olympics, former Olympic skater Scott Hamilton served as one of the commentators for the ice skating events. At one point, Hamilton shared about his special relationship with his mother, who had died prior to his winning an Olympic gold medal.

"The first time I skated in the U.S. Nationals, I fell five times," Hamilton said. "My mother gave me a big hug and said, 'It's only your first National. It's no big deal.' My mother always let me be me. Three years later I won my first National. She never said, 'You can do better,' or 'Shape up.' She just encouraged me."

The key word for communicating as a good gardener-parent is: "encourage."

Empowering, Maturing

Our job as parents is to empower our children to become mature. Maturity can imply many things, but basically it's the ability to contribute to the good of other people in a positive and constructive way. Perhaps this definition is best illustrated in 1 Thessalonians 5:11, where we are instructed to "encourage one another and build each other up" *(NIV)*. We want our children to grow up knowing how to love and serve people and how to assist them in their growth.

Most children don't develop these characteristics of maturity on their own. They must be empowered to maturity through the guidance of their parents. Jack and Judith Balswick describe the concept of empowering so well:

> Parents who are empowerers will help their children become competent and capable persons, who will in turn empower others. Empowering parents will be actively and intentionally engaged in various pursuits—teaching, guiding, caring, modeling—which will equip their children to become confident individuals able to relate to others. Parents who empower will help their children recognize the strengths and potentials within and find ways to enhance these qualities. Parental empowering is the affirmation of the child's ability to learn, grow, and become all that one is meant to be as part of God's image and creative plan.[7]

Parental love that is empowering *en*ables rather than *dis*ables a child.

Tony Campolo's son Bart described how his mother raised him:

> Mom had a different way of helping me figure things out, and that really helped me when I was trying on all of those different identities as a kid. It was quite simple, really, and it grew out of her characteristically unlimited optimism. No matter what I was into at the time, she always managed to see some marvelous way in which I could use it to do good.
>
> When I was a "jock," she talked with great excitement about how I might become the kind of coach who makes a difference in the lives of his players. When I ran with kids who were in trouble, she used to speculate on what was troubling them and how I could use my influence to get them back on track. As a high school freshman, I became obsessed with juggling for awhile, which seemed like a pretty neutral thing to me. Not to Mom, though. "Oh Bart!" she bubbled. "Imagine all the joy you could bring to people in old folks homes and hospitals as a juggler. That would be so exciting!" She even bought me a set of special juggling pins and rings to spur me on.
>
> The genius of her enthusiasm was that it never depended on what I was doing—she found glorious possibilities in everything I tried. Her unspoken message was very clear to me at the time: I was free to become anything I chose to be because no matter what I did, it could and must be done for God and for the good of His people.
>
> That's what real freedom is, I think: the understanding that in a world filled with choices and decisions, under tremendous pressure from other people and our own desires, amid the paralyzing fear of mistakes or failure, loving God and loving His people are the only things that really matter, and doing those things is a decision that we

genuinely have the ability to make in every situation.

You and Mom didn't let me do whatever I wanted to, Dad, but you gave me my freedom nonetheless. I think I finally appreciate it.

Love, Bart[8]

The Architect-Parent

Another way to look at a parent's role is as an architect—but not all the characteristics are productive.

Have you ever seen an architect at work? He goes to the drawing board and, in very intricate detail, designs the end product, whether a new home or a shopping mall. Many parents today are like architects in their parenting style. They believe they are totally responsible for what the child becomes.

God is the One who has in mind the true and ultimate goal and purpose for our children. In reality, He is the architect; we must yield to His design.

Architect-parents mentally design all aspects of their child's life, including the end product. They have a clear and definite picture of what they want their child to become. They carefully guide and control their child's activities, choices and relationships. They screen what he is exposed to, and make sure he plays and socializes with the "right" children. The words "ought" and "should" are frequently heard in an architect-controlled family.

We all have a tendency to mold our children to match the design we have for their lives. If their unique tendencies threaten us, we try to make these differences disappear. We unwittingly attempt to fashion our children into a revised edition of ourselves. We want them to be created in our own image.

Even when the child has reached adulthood, architect-parents' expectations may continue to operate. They may still try to select a child's vocation and the kind of person he will marry. If the parents are successful in achieving their goals, they will probably end up with a highly dependent adult child who is riddled with guilt at every turn. He may be spiritually indecisive and weak, having a distorted perspective of God. The attainment of an architect-parent's goal can carry a high cost, both to the adult child and to the parents themselves. For these are the parents who often experience the big three: burnout, frustration and anger.

Unfortunately, the key word for the communication style of the architect-parent is "dictate," because such parents often establish themselves as dictators in their children's lives. Parental communication is almost always a directive of some kind: when and where not to go, what and what not to do and say, and so on. And the pattern often continues into adulthood.

Our role as a parent is not to supersede God's plan by interfering with His purpose and design. He is the One who has in mind the true and ultimate goal and purpose for our children. In reality, He is the architect; we must yield to His design.[9]

Even with all its potential dangers, the role of the architect-parent is not useless in contributing to a child's maturity and independence. The empowering techniques of *telling* and *teaching*, which are vital to a child's first three or four years of growth, are often best served by this role.

Problems arise, however, when the architect mentality dominates the parenting of older children and adolescents who need more room to think and decide for themselves. Perhaps it will help to remember these twin truths about relinquishment: the tighter you hold on in order to keep your son, the more he will pull away from you; and the greater the amount of relinquishment you give, the more he will draw close to you.

Combining the Roles

The parenting role I like to suggest is a combination of all the above. As we learn who our child is, and diligently explore and discover his unique qualities and gifts, we must cultivate and nurture his individuality without forcing him to become something he is not. A modified architectural approach can be implemented in the process, as long as the plans are flexible and custom-fitted to each child.[10]

Choices and Consequences

As early as possible, let your son experience the result of natural and logical consequences. Talk with him before he tries new experiences, and use this approach when you correct him. Ask him what he thinks might occur if he makes certain choices. Involve him in the decision-making process. Give him several possibilities from which to choose. As he grows older, give him more and more of a voice in family decisions. Encourage his decision-making ability, and let him know you believe in his capability. The belief you have in his potential and his giftedness will in time become his own belief about himself.

But you also have to be willing to let him experience consequences. You cannot always rescue him, as much as you may want to. It will be up to you to teach him how to turn negative experiences and failure into learning experiences. I like the way the authors of *Parenting Teens with Love and Logic* express this principle:

> One of the ironies of parenting is that the best way to influence teens to become irresponsible and fail at life is to become highly involved in making sure that they *do* make it. This is because the implied message in that involvement is, "I don't think you're going to succeed, so I'd better get in here." And the teen lives up to that.
>
> Overly involved parents who intrude on their children's lives from kindergarten through twelfth grade will

almost always raise learning-resistant children.

To help your teen, and give yourself a break in the process, follow these four steps to responsible offspring:

STEP 1: Give your teen a responsibility.

STEP 2: Trust that your teen will carry it out, and at the same time hope and pray that he blows it. Because that's how he'll learn the most from it. If he blows it today, there's a learning experience at the end of it.

Of course, hoping he'll blow it doesn't mean you'll be sending messages that he's worthless and can't think for himself. It's just that the cost of his mistakes is cheaper today than he will ever have to pay to learn that lesson in the real world.

STEP 3: When he does blow it, stand back and allow consequences to occur while expressing empathy.

STEP 4: This is the most important one: Turn right around and give him that same responsibility all over again, because that sends the powerful implied message, "You're so smart that you can learn. People do learn from their mistakes, and you're no different. I'm sure you'll learn from yours, too."

That beats the parent who criticizes by communicating, "You blew it! Now I have to do it." The powerful implied message here is, "You're so dumb you can't learn from what happened."[11]

*P*lanting Roots, Sprouting Wings

The older your son becomes, the less influence you will have on him. For a number of years you were intertwined with your son as part of his root system. The roots will always be there. But hopefully he's added some wings so he can survive on his own. Part of his calling from God is to become the next generation. His task is to sprout wings;

yours (and his father's) is to let go and encourage him to fly.

Let's face it. We all have our dreams of what we want our children to be. We have high hopes for them. If we believe strongly in our value system and our faith, why wouldn't we want our children to reflect the same! If we believe in the ethic of hard work and honesty, of course we want our children to be somewhat of a replica. This is natural.

Unfortunately, however, it doesn't always turn out that way. And when it doesn't, it's easy to pick up the parental reins once again so that we can create a course correction. But it won't work. Instead, we must alter our expectations. My wife and I have had to do that with our own children.

Test Cases

How will you handle it if your son does any of the following?

He may choose a church of a different denomination or a different faith, or even renounce what he was taught.

He may become a member of a cult or a radical, militant "right-wing" organization.

He may give up a prestigious job to live in the back woods of Alaska, join the Peace Corps or become a missionary to China. (If it's the latter, you may only see him every four years because of the missionary rotation system.)

He may not finish college or even high school, and choose to work repairing cars in the service station in your neighborhood.

He may live with a girlfriend, become a father out of wedlock, marry a woman who is not a Christian or is of another race.

He may choose to drive a motorcycle to work rather than a car. (This is the case with some of our friends. The boy's mother wakes up every day very early in the morning to pray when he is riding on the freeway.)

Your son (or his wife) may choose not to have any children or be unable to have any and adopt a multiracial child.

Your son may drink excessively or become addicted to drugs.

I have seen every one of these scenarios occur within families.

Grieving and Recovery

Letting go of expectations is a form of loss. It is a process that must include grieving over that loss if recovery and adjustment are to occur. The greater the intensity of your expectations and the greater the hope for their fulfillment, the greater will be the sense of loss.

Part of the difficulty with our parental expectations is that they come out of the emptiness of our own need for fulfillment, family history and tradition, and society's standards, rather than seeking the face of God and His will for who and what a son is to become. Prayers for a son are not a memo to God telling Him of our plans. They are seeking His plan for both mother and son.

One of the expectations I had to give up was seeing my daughter attend and graduate from college. I completed nine years of college, so I just naturally assumed my children would also attend college, following my pattern. But it was not to be. After a year at Biola University our daughter quit, became a manicurist, and for a few months attended an art college.

Our son Matthew never attended any regular school because of his profound retardation. Because his condition was discovered during the first year of his life, many expectations and dreams never materialized. That was a loss in itself. Out of necessity we had to alter our future hopes for our son, and to learn to accept any sign of slight improvement as an answer to prayer and a blessing from God.

It is far better for you to adjust the expectations you have for your son and experience loss over them than it is to hold on to your expectations and lose your relationship with your son. The latter loss could linger on for years; in some cases I have seen, it is permanent. Some mistakes can be corrected and some cannot.

Mad About Maturity

Nancy was in her early 50s. Her only son had been born when she was 36. He was 17 now, preparing to leave home; and it was a difficult time for both of them.

"I'm not sure if my age has anything to do with my problems," she said, "or if this is just a normal process. I want Jim to grow up, but the more I think about it the madder I get.

"I wanted children for so many years, and finally I have a son. Ten years later his father leaves, but I think 'I still have Jim.' And now just before I hit 60, I'm losing Jim, in a sense. So what do I do now? All I see is being alone and at 65 I'll have to retire. I wish I could slow the whole process down a bit."[12]

Nancy isn't the only one who has these feelings.

Relinquishing a son can be especially difficult if he happens to have been a problem child, or if he's the last one to leave home. If you feel you have failed in some way, it adds to the sense of discomfort.

Sometimes when a son leaves home, a mixture of both pain and relief are present. A 44-year-old mother of five, married 25 years to a maintenance man, shared her feelings about her son's leaving home:

> It hurts that he's gone because things are terrible between us now, and he doesn't come around much anymore. But, I don't know, I think it's better since he's gone. It's a relief not to have to see him every day. Oh, I don't know. What can I say? It hurts not to see him, but it hurts more to see him and be reminded."[13]

Lillian Rubin, who recorded this woman's thoughts, notes the pain in her words and remarks that it reflects the belief that the woman had failed as a mother, and looks back on the past with regret. Furthermore, the woman was stuck with a sense of incompleteness, feeling that her life's work was not finished but is now out of her control. Rubin concludes:

> It's somewhat akin to having to deal with the death of a parent with whom conflicts remain unresolved. The departing child is not dead, of course. But the psychological experience of the loss can be the same. Psycho-

logically, it feels like it's the last chance to heal the divisions, the last chance to make peace. Thus, just as in a death, the departure of a child with whom there is conflict means that the loss is experienced more keenly, the grief more difficult to manage and work through.[14]

From the Son's Viewpoint

But let's consider the other side of the coin. It may be difficult for you as a parent to go through the progressive process of releasing your son. But it can be just as traumatic for him, although he is looking forward to being on his own. The experience can contain a mixture of joy and fear. To stand on your own and be a separate person can take a large amount of emotional energy.

This is why adolescence can be so trying...for everyone. Teenagers experiment and try various ways and approaches to being an adult. It's also a time of mistakes, and of trial and error for everyone. A part of becoming an adult is making decisions without your parents. A mother's task at this time is not to resist this process, but to help. And the way you help is by working on resolving some issues together, and allowing your son to resolve some issues by himself.

Beyond Our Fondest Hopes

It is unusual for a mother (or a father) to have a fully developed life script for their son. Unfortunately, some do; but it won't work. It is common, however, for a mother to hope her son creates a life for himself that meets or exceeds some of her basic expectations. A parent wants this for a number of reasons.

If a son's life is going forward and he's doing all right in his work or marriage, then a mother doesn't have to worry about her son and his future.

If a son is doing well, a mother feels comfortable in responding to her friends' questions about him. She's not embarrassed about her reply.

If a son is doing well, a mother feels better about her role as a parent. If he isn't, she may feel it's her fault and that others think so, too.

If a son is doing well, a mother may have a sense of satisfaction that she has accomplished something extra in her life. Parents often gain satisfaction from vicariously living through their child.

If a son is doing well, it's possible for him to understand and relate more easily to his mother—especially if their goals and values are similar. Conflict tends to be lessened.

If a son is doing well, he may feel greater validation from you and therefore show his appreciation for you.[15]

Rites—and Rights—of Passage

Every society has rites of passages—rituals and ceremonies and events that mark important stages in life. In the upper echelons of our society, daughters are "presented" at a "coming out ball." It's an event recognizing her age and entrance into new events in her life.

Traditionally, weddings have been a rite of passage. The bride walks down the aisle on her father's arm. When they reach the altar, they stop. Her father steps back, as she steps forward and joins the groom. When the wedding ceremony is over, the girl who had entered with her father leaves with the groom. Within a few minutes time, she is transformed from a girl who was dependent upon her father into a grown-up married woman. The boy she marries is supposed to be a man now—an adult who is ready to assume the responsibilities of a family.

College graduations fall into the same category. When it's over, the graduate is now supposed to be ready for the adult world of employment. That is, if he can find a job.

Years ago these events had more significance than they do today. Both the child and the parents usually experienced a sense of relief and satisfaction. It used to be that the parents' task was to raise their child (or children), launch them to become responsible adults, go through the empty-nest syndrome until they were provided with grandchildren, and eventually watch the process repeat itself again.

Today, instead of distinct lines between adolescence and adulthood, we see a blurring. The sequence of these ceremonies is not on the same schedule. The economy often dictates against some of the adult transitions to which many people became accustomed. Adult children marry later, don't leave home for years, then after finally leaving they often return home to save money.

Marking Rites of Passage

The letter from a woman to her prospective daughter-in-law, which I shared in a previous chapter, is a good example of how we can make the rite of passage called marriage a smoother trip. Perhaps we mothers and fathers should consider similar letters to our children, or a

A rite-of-passage letter could contain several elements, including your hopes and dreams for your son, what you expect of him at this stage of his life, and what he can expect from you.

series of letters at different stages, marking events and clarifying new freedoms and responsibilities. I have heard of many parents who write such letters at graduation, and when the son or daughter becomes 21.

A rite-of-passage letter could contain several elements, including your hopes and dreams for your son, what you expect of him at this stage of his life and what he can expect from you.

If he is leaving home, you might write a letter containing parting advice or admonition. Perhaps you could also share your belief in what an adult son is, and how, if and when he marries, his wife will become the significant woman in his life. You might share your belief in his ability to make it as an adult son.

Some mothers and fathers (unfortunately, not enough) talk with their adolescents and prepare them years in advance for the economic realities of life. One of the reasons for doing this is to let them know that at a certain time they are on their own, and will not be dependent upon their parents. When economic dependence exists, we usually find emotional dependence as well.

Recently, I discovered an example of the kind of letter I've been describing. Stu Weber and his wife, Linda, presented the letter to their son as they released him into adulthood. They were meeting their son, appropriately enough, at Lexington Green, the famous "Birthplace of Freedom" at Lexington, Massachusetts, not far from where "the shot heard 'round the world" marked the beginning of the Revolutionary War.

The Webers decided to "fire" one of their own shots, and prayed it would have significant influence as a symbol of their son's "graduation" from home. They wrote their message on a sheet of parchment and framed it. It read:

> "As arrows in the hand of a warrior, so are the children of one's youth. How blessed is the man whose quiver is full of them."
>
> To a world very much needing his character, his gifts, his skill, and his love for Christ, we, Stu and Linda Weber, do proudly and humbly announce in the manner of our heavenly Father, this is our beloved son, Kent Byron Weber, in whom we are well pleased. Like an arrow fashioned not to remain in the quiver, but to be released into the heart of its target, we release Kent to adulthood. We know him to be thoughtful, capable, and mature. He is the message we release to a world we will never see. He is a man. We release him to his manhood and all of its responsibilities. To the finding and cherishing of a godly

and supportive wife, to the begetting and raising by God's grace and design of believing children. And to the commission of the Lord Jesus Christ Himself to go into all the world, making followers of all people, teaching them to observe the rich and life-giving truths of His holy scriptures. Kent, we love you, we're extremely proud of you, and we release you to the target of being all you can be in Christ. You will always be our son. You will never again be our little boy. Thank you, Kent, for having graced our lives with your remarkable sonship. You have blessed us richly.

"Be strong, therefore, and show yourself a man" (1 Kings 2:2).

"Be on the alert, stand firm in the faith, act like men, be strong. Let all that you do be done in love" (1 Corinthians 16:13).

Your very fulfilled parents,
Stu and Linda Weber,
Mom and Dad, Spring 1992[16]

Reflecting on This Chapter

1. In what way do (or did) you teach your children by asking non-threatening questions?

In what way does (or did) your spouse do this with your children?

2. In what way do (or did) you try to see exciting possibilities in things in which your son shows interest?

In what way does (or did) your spouse do this with your son?

3. In what way do (or did) you serve as your son's teacher?

   In what way does (or did) your spouse do this with your son?

4. In what ways have you already begun the process of relinquishing and empowering your young child?

   If you have not yet begun, at what age would it be appropriate to start, and in what ways?

5. In what ways can adolescents be relinquished, and helped to accept responsibilities and consequences?

6. In what ways, and when, did your own parents begin to relinquish you as a teenager?

7. Name some ways your parents fully relinquished, or failed to relinquish, you as an adult.

8. How has your child fulfilled your expectations?

   Exceeded them?

   Disappointed you?

9. What has been or is the greatest barrier to relinquishing your child?

10. To what degree do you accept who your son is at this time in his life?

11. Are you aware of some way your children do not feel you have relinquished them?

12. What are the positive characteristics of your relationship with your son or daughter now?

13. What are the negative characteristics of your relationship with your children now?

14. What could you do now to improve your relationship with your son or relinquish him even more?

Recommended Reading:
Stephen Bly, *Just Because They've Left Home Doesn't Mean They're Gone* (Colorado Springs, CO: Focus on the Family, 1993).

Notes
1. James Dobson, *Parenting Isn't for Cowards* (Dallas, TX: WORD Inc., 1987), pp. 209-211.
2. Jerry and Mary White, *When Your Kids Aren't Kids Anymore* (Colorado Springs, CO: NavPress, 1989), pp. 20-21. (This book is no longer printed in the United States but by Scripture Press of England, under the

title, *When Your Child Isn't a Child Anymore*, 1990).
3. Ibid., pp. 22-23.
4. Ibid.
5. Ibid., p. 42.
6. H. Norman Wright, *The Power of a Parent's Words* (Ventura, CA: Regal Books, 1991).
7. Jack O. Balswick and Judith K. Balswick, *The Family* (Grand Rapids, MI: Baker Book House, 1979), pp. 22-23.
8. Tony and Bart Campolo, *Things We Wish We Had Said* (Dallas, TX: WORD Inc., 1989), pp. 62-63.
9. Ralph Mattson and Thom Black, *Discovering Your Child's Design* (Elgin, IL: David C. Cook, 1989), pp. 189-191.
10. Wright, *The Power of a Parent's Words*, chapters 9-13.
11. Foster Cline and Jim Fay, *Parenting Teens with Love and Logic* (Colorado Springs, CO: Piñon Press, 1992), pp. 139-140.
12. Shauna Smith, *Making Peace with Your Adult Children* (New York: Harper Perpennial, 1991), pp. 324-327.
13. Lillian B. Rubin, *Women of a Certain Age* (New York: HarperCollins, 1979), pp. 22-23.
14. Ibid., p. 23.
15. Lynn Osterkamp, *How to Deal with Your Parents* (New York: Berkley Books, 1992), p. 37.
16. Stu Weber, *Tender Warrior* (Sisters, OR: Questar, 1993), pp. 166-167.

When Your Sons Are Grown

IF YOU ARE THE MOTHER OF A YOUNG SON, PROJECT YOURSELF TO A TIME IN THE future when he will be an adult. What elements of your parenting style today can you predict will show up in his life as a grown person?

If your son is already grown, what elements in the way you raised him can you see in his life today?

Back to the Future

As a younger parent, can you see yourself in any of the following scenarios in the future? As a parent of an adult son, do any of these scenes seem familiar?

Jean, a 57-year-old mother, struggled with her relationship with her adult son. In tears, she described her present relationship. "It's been over a year since I've seen Jim. I just don't understand why it's so difficult for us to get together. We only live two hours apart. We were so close when he was growing up, and I think it was healthy. I don't think I push myself on him. I've tried to keep my distance, but I feel cut off and abandoned. I've asked if there's a problem, but I just don't seem to get a response. I feel rejected. Do you have any suggestions?"

Michelle, in her mid-40s, was angry when she came in for her appointment. In fact, she was steaming! "All we do is argue, argue, argue," she said. "That son of mine won't take any advice, especially since he married that girl. She is so unfriendly. I know we're a loud, expressive family and we speak our mind, but she could learn to do the same. She's like a mouse when she comes over for our monthly family get-together. You know, I've got a lot more experience and more life behind me than the two of them put together, so I don't know why they can't take advantage of it and listen for a change. I need some help on this."

Eva was a quiet, elderly lady who had three sons in their 40s. Her concern was a bit different. "I wonder if I did the best I could with my sons," she said. "I hope I helped them become good fathers to their children. They seem to be doing all right, but I wonder if they're really happy with me. They never complain, and we see each other a lot. We get together every Christmas and for my birthday, but we do the same thing year after year. Sometimes I wonder if they would like to make some changes, but they're just too polite to say anything. Is there anything I can do to find out what they really think?"

Many mothers of an adult son struggle with their relationship with him (and often with his wife). It can continue for years. At least the three mothers in the previous examples were sharing their questions and concerns with someone who might be fairly objective.

It is possible to take some steps that will improve a distant or hostile relationship, or make a healthy one even better. But if you are a mother, you will need to take the initiative and make the initial concessions in order to make this work. It's the best way to eliminate defensiveness on the son's part.

Toward Harmonious Relationships

Scripture calls us to live in harmony, peace and love—especially in our families.

> He who is steadfast in righteousness—uprightness and right standing with God—shall attain to life, and he who pursues evil does it to his own death (Prov. 11:19).

> Finally, brethren, farewell—rejoice! Be strengthened—perfected, completed, made what you ought to be; be encouraged and consoled and comforted; be of the same (agreeable) mind one with another; live in peace, and [then] the God of love [Who is the Source]—of affection, goodwill, love and benevolence toward men—and the Author and Promoter of peace will be with you (2 Cor. 13:11).

> Let all bitterness and indignation and wrath (passion, rage, bad temper) and resentment (anger, animosity) and quarreling (brawling, clamor, contention) and slander (evilspeaking, abusive or blasphemous language) be banished from you, with all malice (spite, ill will or baseness of any kind). And become useful and helpful and kind to one another, tenderhearted (compassionate, understanding, lovinghearted), forgiving one another [readily and freely], as God in Christ forgave you (Eph. 4:31,32).

> And let the peace (soul harmony which comes) from the Christ rule (act as umpire continually) in your hearts—

deciding and settling with finality all questions that arise in your minds—[in that peaceful state] to which [as members of Christ's] one body you were also called [to live]. And be thankful—appreciative, giving praise to God always (Col. 3:15).

Imperfect Parents

How do you begin? First of all, you acknowledge the fact that you are not a perfect parent. Neither do you have perfect children. They are imperfect now, and they will be as adults.

We all have the ability to behave both well, as well as badly. As the parent of an adult child you will not want to waste time blaming yourself, your husband or your son. Blaming is easy, because it's one way to make sense of what doesn't make sense, and it helps to get the responsibility off of ourselves. But blaming is not productive.

Reflecting on Your Role

Perhaps the next step is to reflect on your role as a parent in raising your son or daughter. I would like you to take the time to answer these questions in detail before you continue reading.

1. Describe the home in which you were raised.
2. How was your past home similar to the home atmosphere in which you are raising your own children?
3. What trauma did you experience as you were raised?
4. What trauma may your young son be experiencing as you raise him?
5. What are (were) your strengths as a parent?
6. What are your weaknesses as a parent?
7. What are your son's strengths?
8. What are your son's (or daughter's) weaknesses?
9. Do you have a dream for your son's life?

10. What type of relationship do you want with your son now, at his present age?
11. How would your son like your relationship to change?
12. What can you do at this time to make this a reality?
13. What type of relationship do you envision having with your son when he is grown?

Understanding Adult Sons

As you consider building a new relationship with your adult son-to-be, or the adult son you have now, remember to keep in mind what was discussed in an earlier chapter about personality differences. You must approach your son in a way that both respects his uniqueness and enables him to hear you.

Try to project yourself into your son's life and mind, and discover what he might be thinking and feeling. I think most mothers try to give their sons what they need and want. The problem is, your son may have a completely different idea of his needs and wants.

What Adult Sons Fear Most

In talking with some adult sons, we have been able to identify some of the issues they struggle with in their relationship with their mother. Unfortunately, some sons live more with fear of their mother than with closeness. The following statements reflect these fears. Could your young son voice these fears? Could your adult son be living with any of them?

One adult son: "I guess what I'm afraid of is disappointing my mom. She expects so much of me that I'm really careful what I tell her about my life. If I make any kind of a change in my life, I just wait until I'm settled again and then I tell her about it. It's not worth the hassle."

Another son: "I've learned to be as noncommittal as possible. If I have a strong opinion about something and it goes counter to Mom's view, the *onslaught of anger* begins. I can't handle that intense conflict. I admit it. I'm an avoider."

Yet another: "If there is one thing I can't handle, it's hurting Mom. And she's such a worrier! I'd like to share some of my struggles with her, but it just overwhelms her and I feel so bad when she's hurt. I wish she could handle it better."

You've heard about large companies that take over other companies? That's exactly what Mom does if you give her any chance."

Another: "You know what hurts? It's being put down and *rejected.* It tears me up, and I never know when it's going to happen. I've learned not to say too much, but then I get dumped on for that. It's easy to figure out why I don't visit much anymore."

And another: "You've heard about large companies that take over other companies? That's exactly what Mom does if you give her any chance. I'm a pretty talented person, but not in her eyes. She always has to *take over* what I'm doing and drown me with advice."

The fear of disappointing Mom, experiencing her anger, hurting her, being rejected by her and being taken over by her are all too common.

The Generation Gap

Family relationships face a generation difference in terms of values, needs, beliefs and desires. In each successive generation these differences seem to crop up more rapidly. Mothers (and fathers) tend to see less of a gap than adult sons do. Parents tend to minimize the differences, as well as to want more emotional closeness. Parents usually see better communication and understanding in a relationship than their children do. An adult child seems to feel freer to describe dissatisfactions in his relationship with his parents than do his parents.

A study was done of 513 people who have one or more children and at least one living parent. It is interesting to note the responses of these adult children.

They expressed significantly more dissatisfactions in their relationship with their parents than with their own children.

They tended to say they enjoyed being with their own children more than with their parents.

They tended to say they had a better relationship with their children than with their parents.

And they were more likely to say they found their children less annoying than their parents.[1]

What we may think is something special for our child may be totally missing the mark because we respond out of our experience, rather than discovering what our son needs.

Roles Family Members Play

Sometimes, in a family that doesn't function well, three different roles are acted out. I'm not recommending them, in fact, I suggest they be avoided at all costs. But it may be helpful for you to ask yourself whether they are present in your own family.

Some member in a family may take the role of a *victim*. This leads to a feeling of having no power or influence. Did or do you feel like a victim? Does or did your son feel like a victim?

Another role is that of the *persecutor*. This person ends up acting and feeling like a bad guy. Did or do you feel like a persecutor? Did or does your son?

Another common role we hear much about today is the *rescuer*. They constantly snatch others out of difficulty, and they may do so in a sacrificial and noble way.[2]

If you see any of these roles being played out, change is needed. You must learn to respond to your child as an honest, open, mature adult—not in a role that does damage.

Rebuilding a Relationship

Parents of adult sons may have mixed feelings about attempting to change or rebuild the relationship. It can be risky as well as scary, but it is certainly worth the effort. I think most adult sons would like a healthy, positive relationship with their mother. The problem is, someone has to take the first step. If your son is not yet an adult, can you envision yourself taking this step?

Crucial Questions

One mother answered the previous 13 questions and also sent them to her son prior to a visit. She said that she had answered the questions, and would be interested in how he would answer them. She said she was looking forward to hearing his perspective.

Another mother asked her son the question, "Do you really know me and why I am the way I am?" She then proceeded to ask him to answer the following 46 questions as he thought they would apply to her. He could ask her about any questions he could not answer, and discuss any of them further in order to discover whether his information and perceptions were accurate.

1. What special memories do you have about your childhood? (Remember: these were asked by the adult son to his adult mother, the idea being to see how well he knows his mom.)
2. How did you get along with each of your parents? What were they like?
3. What did you like and dislike about your parents?
4. What was your most pleasant and most unpleasant experience with each parent?
5. What were your hurts and disappointments as a child?
6. What were your hobbies and favorite games?
7. How did you usually get into trouble?
8. How did you usually try to get out of trouble?

9. What did you enjoy about school and its activities?
10. What pets did you have? Which were your favorites and why?
11. What did you dream about doing when you were older?
12. Did you like yourself as a child? Why or why not?
13. Did you like yourself as a teenager? Why or why not?
14. What were your talents and special abilities?
15. What awards and special achievements did you win?
16. Did you have a nickname?
17. Who were your close friends? Where are they today?
18. What would you do on a hot summer afternoon?
19. Describe the area where you grew up—people, neighborhood, etc.
20. What were you afraid of? Do you have any of those fears today?
21. How did you get along with your brothers and/or sisters? If you had none, which relative were you closest to?
22. Who did you date and for how long? Where did you go on dates?
23. How did you feel when you liked someone and that person didn't care for you?
24. What was your spiritual life like as a child? As an adolescent?
25. How has being an adult changed your life?
26. How are you different today than you were 20 years ago? Ten years ago?
27. What have been your greatest disappointments? How have you handled them?
28. What have you learned from them that you would want me to learn?
29. If you could live your life over again, what would you do differently?
30. What do you want to be remembered for?
31. How did you meet my dad?
32. What was your first impression of him?
33. What was happening in your lives at the time you met?
34. How did your parents respond to your dating and engagement? How did his parents respond?

35. How did you make the decision to marry? Who proposed and how?
36. What have been the strengths and weaknesses of your marriage?
37. How did you get along with your in-laws at first?
38. How did you feel when you were expecting me?
39. What was it like to have children? How did it change your life?
40. What did you like and dislike about being parents?
41. What are your general impressions of me as a person?
42. What are your hopes and dreams for me?
43. What about me has brought you the greatest satisfaction? The greatest disappointment?
44. How have I changed as an adult?
45. How would you like me to grow and develop at this stage of my life?
46. In what way am I most like you? In what way am I least like you?[3]

Listening Through Difficulties

As you reflect upon these questions, which of them might be difficult for you to discuss with your adult son? Some of them could elicit unpleasant feelings. If so, how do you think you would handle them in a way that would still enable you to interact with your son? In addition to the questions listed, what else do you think would be important for him to know about you?

If you give your son these 46 questions, don't let any defensiveness on your part raise a barrier. You may not hear what you want to hear. The answers may hurt. You need to keep in mind that your value and worth is not based upon your son's perception, or on how well you did as a parent. You may feel that his perception is wrong, distorted or exaggerated; but just listen.

Remember the difference between hearing your son and *listening* to him. Hearing is basically to gain content or information for your own purposes. Listening is caring for and being empathic toward the person who is talking. Hearing means that you are concerned about what is going on inside *you* during the conversation. Listening means you are trying to understand the feelings of *the other person,* and to listen for his sake.

Here is a threefold definition of listening. Listening means that when your son is talking to you:

1. You are not thinking about what you are going to say when he stops talking. You are not busy formulating your response. You are concentrating on what is being said and are putting into practice Proverbs 18:13: "He who answers a matter before he hears the facts, it is folly and shame to him."

2. You are completely accepting of what is being said, without judging what he says or how he says it. You may fail to hear the message if you are thinking that you don't like your son's tone of voice or the words he is using. You may react on the spot to the tone and content, and miss the meaning. Perhaps he hasn't said it in the best way, but why not listen and then come back later when both of you are calm, and then discuss the proper wording and tone of voice? Acceptance does not mean you have to agree with the content of what is said. Rather, it means that you understand that what your son is saying is something he feels.

3. You can repeat what your son has said and what you think he was feeling while speaking to you. Real listening implies an obvious interest in his feelings and opinions and an attempt to understand them from his perspective.

God's Word gives us directives concerning how we are to listen:

> Any story sounds true until someone tells the other side
> and sets the record straight (Prov. 18:17, *TLB*).

> The wise man learns by listening; the simpleton can learn
> only by seeing scorners punished (Prov. 21:11, *TLB*).

> Let every man be quick to hear (a ready listener) (Jas.
> 1:19).

Communicating Through Pain

If you are trying to reestablish a relationship with a son that has been estranged, be prepared for some painful moments. I have seen some encounters in which the son literally dumped his accumulated anger of years onto his mother without fully realizing the intensity or devastating effect. I don't want to alarm you, but it has happened.

Keep in mind that underneath your son's concern is very possibly a desire for a closer, more loving, more fulfilling and harmonious relationship. Sons of all ages still want their mother's love and approval. They want to be seen and heard, which includes having their perspective and feelings acknowledged and validated. If the relationship was a painful, difficult experience, then usually a son wants the opportunity to express his anger and to hear acknowledgment and recognition on the part of his mother.

In some families, sons grow up never fully knowing their mother and father because neither one has opened up and shared how they felt. Thoughts were there but feelings were absent. Discussions like these give an opportunity to honestly share feelings in an objective manner. But once again, remember how important it is to package your responses in a way that fits your son's communication and learning style.

Sharing the Responsibility

If your relationship was or is a problem, both parties have contributed to the difficulty. Most of the married couples I counsel come to the sessions having each spouse believing he or she is more innocent than their partner. Often it's the same with a parent and adult child as well. What each party is looking for is to have the other party express regret over the pain, distress or situation they have experienced Your son may be looking for this from you.

It may take you awhile to be able to identify your feelings or responsibility. You don't have to agree fully with your son's perception, but you can say, "I'd like to think about what you've said for a while. I think there could be something to what you've said, and I need to reflect upon it." This is a nondefensive response, and it keeps the door open for continuing the discussion.

As it is possible for anyone to have done better at any task, it is possible to make some form of admission. This does not discount the fact that you may have a mixture of feelings at this time.

Taking the First Step

Often a son is hoping to hear what a mother will do immediately to improve the relationship. He will usually be looking for you to make

ℛesist responding, "You were a difficult child to handle. It wasn't easy." This sort of counterattack quickly cuts off communication

some concession, confession or specific change. This doesn't mean that your desire for change in your son's response isn't legitimate. But someone needs to take the first step forward for a relationship to change. We can't sit back and wait for the other person to take the initiative.[4]

Keeping this in mind, here are some responses to *avoid*.

The counterattack. Resist responding, "You were a difficult child to handle. It wasn't easy." This sort of counterattack quickly cuts off communication.

Self-defense. A typical response from a single mother might be: "I tried to be a good mother to you. You don't know how hard it was without a husband. I did what I thought would be best for you and your sisters." But such defensive statements communicate the message, "I don't consider what you're saying to be valid."

Blaming. "You have no idea what your father was like. He's the real reason for the difficulties we experienced as a family. I just wish you really knew." Shifting the blame sends your son the message, "I won't accept any responsibility for the problem."

The Self-Put-Down. "I'm such a failure. I know I wasn't the best mother for you. I can understand why you wouldn't want to be around me." Putting yourself down like this just indicates that you're stuck in the past with no perspective on changing the present or the future.

Discounting. "I don't understand how you could feel that way. That was years ago and I don't know how you could remember that. I can't understand why you're bringing it up now. It just seems you're trying to get back at me and hurt me." Discounting and claiming that your son wants vengeance will probably confirm some of his feelings about the futility of beginning this discussion.

Comparing. "You don't know how good you had it, compared to others. You were given so much. Your father and I just wish we had half the opportunities you did. You never had to worry about having food on the table." Comparing your son's situation with your own sends a message that "your perspective is nothing compared to mine."[5]

Writing About a Relationship

I have worked with many people over the past few years who either sent an initial letter to their son or responded to a letter from him. Sometimes all the interaction takes place through the exchange of letters. Some people find it much easier to begin the process through writing. For one thing, it gives you opportunity to compose and edit. It can also remove the threat of defensiveness, which can be a common problem in face-to-face encounters. Hopefully, the process will progress to phone calls, and, ideally, to a face-to-face discussion.

Following are two different kinds of letters from people I have worked with.

"I Blew It"

The first letter is from a mother who realized that her son had been damaged over the years because of their relationship. Her purpose in writing was to admit her shortcomings, ask for forgiveness and work toward a better relationship. Here is the letter she wrote to her 33-year-old son, whom we'll call Fred:

Dear Fred:

I've had a lot of time to think and reflect about our relationship over the past several months. I've come to the conclusion that one of your favorite phrases that you use does apply to me as a mother. At times, "I blew it." I've realized that I did some things that have hurt and damaged you over the years. I've tried to look at the early years of your life through your eyes and not just my own perspective. I want to try to understand your life from your perspective and not just my own. I may be accurate but if not please let me know where I'm off base. I hope this letter doesn't confuse, hurt, anger or frustrate you, but if it does I can accept that and the responsibility for it. I guess I'm also concerned how you might respond to this. I hope you don't see this as intrusive. Perhaps what I'm saying you wish would have been said years ago. So do I. I don't think I've purposely delayed, but am just now finally understanding clearly what I did or neglected to do.

Here are some of the things I think I did that were wrong and would like to ask your forgiveness for as well as what I intend to do in the future. If you have additional suggestions for me, I would like to hear them.

I am sorry for my intrusion into your personal life and activities during your teenage years and now as an adult. I now realize I probably suffocated you at times. I will keep my suggestions and opinions to myself until you ask for them or tell me it's all right to volunteer them. And when you ask for them they will be tentative, without the words, "You should," and "You must." I am now as bothered about my saying this as you are hearing it.

I am sorry for my anger, which was all too common. I know it not only hurt you but probably confused you as well since sometimes I yelled at you and other times I pulled away and avoided you. You must have felt abandoned at times, too. In the future I will wait until I calm down before I respond and then talk about what's causing my anger. I will not yell, pout, accuse or withdraw.

I'm sorry I used you to experience and have some of the things I didn't have in my own original family as well as in my marriage. I wanted you to achieve and always be the best one. I wanted you to listen as I talked your arm and leg off, since your father wouldn't listen. I will no longer push you. Whatever you do or don't do or however you do it is your choice and yours alone. I love you and accept you for who you are and not for what you achieve. I couldn't always do this. You probably felt you were defective. You weren't. I was. I will condense what I have to say and in your words I will "get to the point" immediately. You can count on it. If it's still too much for you, tell me. I will hear you.

Well, that's it for now. I've left this next section blank so you can fill in what else I did that I need to be aware of and ask forgiveness for. I need you, if you so desire, to complete it and let me know what you would like.

Finally, I leave with you what you would like to do with this letter and when, if you so desire.

I love you,
Mom

Even if the son did not respond, at least this mother would feel better for having taken a positive step forward.

A Charge of Neglect

The second letter is in response to a confrontational letter a mother received from her 25-year-old son. The substance of her son's letter was his resentment toward her, both for "neglect and disinterest" and for times of interference. The interference included his choice of a college, as well as helping to break up an engagement. Here is his mother Lois's response:

> Dear Thad,
>
> I've waited for a week before responding to your letter. I was so hurt and thrown by what you said and the reason is I'm afraid as I look back, it's true. I could give you reasons for what I did but they're really excuses. I know that I hurt you by not showing interest in what you were interested in and my lack of affirming you. How I wish I had! How I wish I knew you better, too. You did know best about which college to attend. And I'm glad you went ahead with what you wanted. I'm just realizing that not only have I hurt you but I've lost out on so much of your life. It's my fault for that. I don't know what to say about Jean. I still have mixed feelings but I realize I really mishandled everything.
>
> I would like to talk more about this if you so desire and when you would like to. I can't change what I did in the past except say I'm sorry and ask your forgiveness. I know also that forgiveness takes time. Is it possible to build a new relationship now? I'm willing to change.
>
> Love,
> Mom

An Unusual Birthday Gift

Sometimes, instead of a letter, a direct meeting can be beneficial. Here is how one mother bravely and successfully asked her children for honest feedback, and made positive changes within her family as a result.[6]

Joanne made phone calls to each of her three adult children, asking them to give her an unusual gift for her birthday. Instead of the cards, gifts, phone calls or dinners they usually gave, she asked them to come over to her home on the Saturday afternoon closest to her birthday. They were to bring the grandchildren who were age 12 and over, and have an open talk about their relationship.

At this meeting, Joanne said openly, "Other people's kids spend time with them, and I don't understand why you don't want to spend time with me. I know it's not my imagination, so please don't tell me that it is. I want to have a better relationship with you and I need to know what the problems are so I can try to correct them."

This meeting was painful in part for Joanne, but also very constructive. When everything was brought out into the open, only three things actually bothered Joanne's children and grandchildren.

The first was her giving them advice when they were not interested in receiving advice.

The second was taking the conversation away from the person speaking. One son showed her how both of these affected him: "When I told you our refrigerator broke down, you interrupted me in the middle of my sentence and told me about how great your refrigerator was and how we should have bought a different brand. I just needed you to listen to me, not tell me about your refrigerator or give me advice."

Another example of how she turned conversations back to herself was given by one of the teenagers, who said, "Well, when I try to talk, you don't listen very well and you tell me the same things that I've heard over and over. I want to listen to you, but it's hard to have a conversation. I don't mean to be rude."

The third problem family members had was that Joanne didn't

understand that when they were busy it was best to leave them alone. For example, her daughter said that when Joanne called and she said they were on the way out, Joanne would ask innumerable questions such as, "Where are you going?" "What are you going to do?" and "How come you're going there?" instead of just saying, "Bye, talk to you later."

It didn't feel great to Joanne to hear these things, but it was a relief to know that specific behaviors of hers were bothering her family, and that it wasn't that they didn't like her as a person. For the first time, she had the option of changing some of these behaviors if she wanted to.

Another thing that became clear during this meeting was that her daughter and her family were extremely busy. The problem was partly a societal and generational time problem that had nothing to do with Joanne personally. Because of their fast-paced and overextended lifestyles, they rarely had time for their own small family units, and didn't include each other in their activities as often as they wanted to.

Additionally, the adolescents in the family were off in their own world a lot of the time, forming their individual identities. The fact that Joanne's friends seemed to have children who spent more time with them was interesting, but didn't necessarily mean their relationship was better. They might be getting together often because they were all trying to avoid conflict. Or that kind of relationship might suit their lifestyle better. It didn't really matter, because what was important was what worked for Joanne's family, not anyone else's.

What will work for you? What steps could you take to initiate a healing in a difficult relationship or to improve a good relationship? As the parent of a younger son, what steps can you take now that might be a midcourse correction in your relationship? It's worth a try.

Reflecting on This Chapter

1. As the mother of a young son, do you see signs either of distance or "clinging" that might be predictors about relational problems when he grows up?

2. What did you learn about yourself as you worked through the list of 13 questions in this chapter?

3. What did you learn about your child/children?

4. What did you learn about your relationship with them?

5. What special things have you done recently for your son that he appreciated?

6. What are some things you have done for your son that he did not seem to appreciate as much as you expected?

7. As the parent of an older or adult son, in what ways are you alike?

   In what ways are you different?

8. Have you ever attempted to rebuild a relationship with your child? Reflecting back on it, what might have been handled differently if you had read this chapter beforehand?

Notes

1. Lynn Osterkamp, *How to Deal with Your Parents* (New York: Berkley Books, 1992), p. 8.
2. Shauna L. Smith, *Making Peace with Your Adult Children* (New York: Harper Perpennial, 1991), pp. 165-169.
3. H. Norman Wright, *Always Daddy's Girl* (Ventura, CA: Regal Books, 1989), pp. 68-70.
4. Smith, *Making Peace with Your Adult Children*, p. 196.
5. Ibid., pp. 187-190.
6. Ibid., pp. 320-321.

chapter

9

"I Never Expected This!"

I<small>T BEGINS WHEN HE IS VERY YOUNG</small>. Y<small>OU HAVE YOUR HOPES, YOUR DREAMS</small>, your expectations for him. You expect a compliant, easygoing boy. Then, at least by the time he is age two, and maybe long before, you see that he definitely has a mind of his own. You wonder about your dreams. And sometimes he turns out to be just the opposite of those early images.

The Shock-and-Frazzle Factor

A friend of mine recounted to me one story after another about the problems he got into unintentionally as a small boy—escapades that would shock and frazzle any mother.

Once he jumped on a freight train to ride to school because he was late and didn't want to walk the three miles. And every afternoon he would swing on a rope from his second-story bedroom window to the neighbor's roof. Neither of these would have been much of a problem except...one day the freight train didn't slow down where it usually did, and he ended up calling his mother from a town 20 miles away.

And one afternoon when he landed on the neighbor's roof, he just kept going and wound up with his legs hanging through the ceiling plaster of their living room!

Another time during the winter he and his friends had been out sledding in the snow all day. It was getting late. The boys were wet, and the temperature was dropping. Their favorite pastime was waiting on a hill for the cars to slow in front of them, and quickly sledding down to grab onto the rear bumper to catch a ride for a block or so.

But two blocks down the hill where they usually let go of the bumper as the cars turned, the boy found he couldn't let go. The drop in temperature had caused his wet gloves to be frozen to the bumper. He was stuck. As the car turned onto a main road, the snow ran out, and sparks flew from the metal runners of the sled as the car picked up speed.

Other drivers could see what was happening, but it wasn't until the driver of the car went through a tunnel that he noticed a stream of sparks following him. When he emerged from the tunnel, he pulled the car over and stopped. By the time he got out and came around to the back of the car, the towed victim had made his escape—leaving behind a pair of frozen gloves hanging from the rear bumper, and a puzzled driver.

When my friend got home late, his mother asked, "Where have you been?"

"Around."

"What were you doing?"

"Oh, nothing much."

"Where are your gloves?"

"I must have left them somewhere."

He went the rest of the winter without gloves. Maybe it's best that moms don't always know every little detail!

Expecting the Unexpected

Perhaps for you it happened when your son came home with a totally different report card than you ever expected. Or when he told you he hated taking piano lessons or playing football. Not *your* son! But it does happen. And finally he reaches adulthood and shows some semblance of stability. Then his marriage fails.

If you are a young mother, you may think that the problems and issues in this chapter only occur in other families, and could not happen in yours. Perhaps they won't. But it is highly unlikely that your son will play out the script you wrote for him. You need to be prepared for a wide range of events. Although they are not your experience, you may be able to reach out and minister to others facing these adjustments. My wife, Joyce, and I, as parents, went through a great deal that we never expected, either. (See *I'll Love You Forever—When a Child Doesn't Meet Your Expectations,* published by Focus on the Family, 1993.)

Parents and the Trauma of Divorce

A major surprise for parents is becoming much more common. More adult children are divorcing. And the shock of discovering that this is happening to an adult son can be especially upsetting and unsettling for Mom.

Perhaps the description of how divorce affects the entire family structure is best described by the authors of *What to Do When Your Son or Daughter Divorces:*

> Just as when your children married you could feel that imaginary string stretch, so when they divorce you can feel

> it shrivel. The family expands and contracts with every
> addition or subtraction of a member. When divorce strikes
> your family, through your child, the alliances and divisions
> throughout the entire extended family shift, even break.
>
> When divorce occurs and you experience so many
> pushes and pulls on near and dear relationships, it is use-
> ful to think of your family as a mobile. If you cut the string
> between any two parts, it unbalances the whole structure,
> until it is repaired. Your whole family reverberates when
> your child divorces and the mobile goes on tilt.[1]

The parents' marriage can sometimes be affected by the different
ways the wife and the husband handle pain and grief. They may have
different ideas about how to respond to their son, to their ex-daughter-in-law, and to her parents.

Upset Value Systems

Parents may feel that their son's divorce threatens their entire value
system. If they are totally opposed to divorce, regardless of the reason,
they will certainly face a difficult time because their sense of values
has been violated. They may struggle more with how to explain it to
others. They may experience guilt if they feel they failed to hand
along their value system to their son.

Parents may discover that the breakup of the marriage is due to
their son's unfaithfulness. Some parents have found it necessary to
deal with diseases such as AIDS in the fallout of their divorcing adult
child. And what will they do if they find out that the marriage failed
because their own son abused his wife?

Anger and Unanswerable Questions

Parents in such situations should be prepared for an onslaught of
anger once the shock of an adult son's impending situation hits them.
They may find themselves brooding over their son's divorce for many

weeks or months. While they are doing the dishes or driving alone, they may fuss and stew about how easily their son and daughter-in-law gave up their marriage. Lives are disrupted by the breakup, and they may have anger at what caused it, who caused it and how all this is affecting everyone involved.

Unanswerable questions arise. "Why didn't they work it out or go for help? Why didn't they see this coming? Why are they giving up so easily? Where's the effort that every marriage takes?" Although parents want to be supportive, a part of them disagrees strongly with what is going on. They begin to worry and wonder how this will affect their son's job, his self-esteem and his financial future.

Parents begin to anticipate all the losses and changes they themselves will experience because of this divorce. Family vacations, family visits, birthdays and holiday gatherings will change. They won't be viewing the video of their son's wedding so often, if at all. And what about the extended vacation they were planning? Does the divorce change all this?

Blame and Guilt

The anger may be accompanied by a need to blame, and they will have a number of targets to vent upon. This could include the in-laws and the attorney. Frequently the parents of a divorcing son begin blaming their spouse for what he or she did or didn't do that contributed to the problem. They may find it helpful to write some nonmailed letters to those with whom they are angry, to help them vent those feelings.

Parents may take some of the guilt and blame on themselves. They begin to take stock of what they did or didn't do, doubting both their adequacy as a parent and as an in-law. If they stayed out of their son and daughter-in-law's life, they may feel they should have been more available. Perhaps more advice would have helped them. They wonder if they couldn't have helped out more financially, spiritually and emotionally. Or perhaps they feel they helped too much, to the point of interfering in their lives.

What About the Grandchildren?

Some pain will center around the struggle and pain of the grandchildren as they try to work through their parents' breakup.

If the adult son is the noncustodial parent, the grandparents will end up losing and hurting more, because they will probably find it more difficult to spend time with the grandchildren. Even if he retains

In a study of freshmen at two major universities, 96 percent said their grandparents were "extremely important" or "important" in their lives.

custody, their concern won't end. They may find it all too easy to fall into the trap of doing too much for the grandchildren, as a way of compensating for their pain and sadness.

In a study of freshmen at two major universities, 96 percent said their grandparents were "extremely important" or "important" in their lives. And 90 percent said they wish they could have spent more time with their grandparents than they did.

All states have visitation laws for grandparents, and grandparents will be able to visit their grandchildren as long as they are able to show that it is in the best interest of the children.

The grandchildren will need plenty of love and acceptance. They need to have confidence in something that gives them stability. Grandparents will be their connection with the past. At first it may feel like walking on eggshells to be around them. The grandparents may be at a loss to know what to say, and they don't know what the grandchildren might ask. The best a grandparent can do is to be available, and to listen. They should let the grandchildren initiate the discussion, and they can check with their adult son to see what the children have been told and what he would like to have said.

As grandparents move into this new and awkward role, they will need to deal both with their own concerns and those of the grandchildren. Will there be enough money to care for them properly? Will they become latchkey children, coming home to an empty house? What if the custodial parent has his or her new romantic interest stay overnight, or, worse, live with them? How will this divorce affect the grandchildren's sense of self-esteem and their academic performance? How will their birthdays, Little League games and trips be handled?

Grandchildren may raise their own concerns and questions, either directly or through their behavior. Suppose you are that grandparent. Here are some common concerns and suggested responses you can make:

1. *"Who will take care of me?"* Reassure them that you can, at intervals or for a period of time. Adolescents need a kind of baby-sitting, too.

2. *"Is there anything in the world reliable and predictable?"* Grandparents should make special efforts to be there for them as promised, every time, barring emergencies. When you say you're going to pick them up or meet them, get there on time. Your reliability is crucial.

3. *"Are my parents crazy?"* When the opportune moment arises, you can explain what an unsettling period this is for both parents, and that after awhile everyone will settle down.

4. *"Where is my father/mother now living?"* Encourage visits to the absent parent's home if that meets with the custody arrangement. The child wants to touch the new base in order to feel part of the new setting.

5. *"Will my mother/father—my only parent—get sick, hit by a car or worse?"* You can't promise this won't happen, but let your grandchild know that you are a backup, and so are the cousins, uncles and aunts from both sides of the family.

6. *"Will we have enough money now?"* Reassure the child that he or she will be taken care of. Perhaps you can help with money or gifts

to your grandchild, giving a weekly allowance or money for a class trip.

7. *"Will I have to change schools now?"* Tell them that many children remain where they are and attend the same school. But if change is in the wind, research the positives in the new school and visit the classroom if you can.

8. *"Will I have to move to a new neighborhood?"* Recount the stories of the times you moved, your new room, new friends and the yard for a dog. If the move is nearby, reassure them that their old friends can visit and stay overnight.

9. *"Is Mom going to marry Bob? Will they keep me with them?"* You probably can't do much about this one except wonder with them.[2]

What About the "Ex-Laws"?

Perhaps one of the most awkward situations is how to relate to your ex-in-laws. Terri, the mother of a newly divorced son told me, "Fred wanted me to cut off all contact with his wife's relatives as he had done. But I told him 'Fred, you may have divorced your wife, but I am not divorcing her mother Ethyl. We've developed a wonderful friendship and prayer partnership over the past 15 years and we have both stated that it will continue. You will just have to learn to accept it.'"

You may always be closer to your son's first set of in-laws than the next set. If you relate better to them and that is your choice, nothing is wrong with that. Or perhaps you never did relate well to your daughter-in-law's parents, and this isn't a major loss for you. You may end up resenting the other grandparents. Some grandparents have also had to go to court to ensure their own visitation rights. But if your son had children in the marriage, you may always have some contact and interaction with them.

If you were especially close to your daughter-in-law, alienation from her will add to your pain. Although she may have destroyed the marriage, you may find it difficult to dislike her if she was the daughter you never had. You feel a push-pull tension and cry out, "Why did this have to happen?"

Refilling the Empty Nest

If your son is a needy or dependent person, you may have more of a struggle because your heart goes out to him and you may end up doing more for him.

It is not uncommon for a divorcing adult child to move back home for financial reasons. This requires adjustments on the part of all concerned. Jay Kesler writes of this situation first from the viewpoint of the adult child:

> When divorced adult children live in the house belonging to their parents, they naturally feel impotent, unable to cope. They feel as if they're not adult; they have failed. As parents of divorced children, we can repeat, "This is working out all right; it isn't a problem; you're not in the way." But still, grown children who are forced to take charity from their own parents feel demeaned and will often react in bizarre and unpredictable ways. Their loss of self-esteem may cause them to engage in withdrawal, in acts of self-denigration, or sometimes even in hostility. They may lash out in anger against the situation, not realizing that they have picked the wrong target. We always hurt the ones we love because they are close to us.[3]

Of course the grandparents have major adjustments to make, too. Perhaps the new arrangement will affect the proposed sale of your home, which used to be too large. It may also change retirement plans. Jay Kesler continues:

> Grandparents can be caught in the middle trying to do the right thing, to be loving and charitable. We often may need to spend a good deal of time in prayer, coming to

terms with understanding our divorced children, forgiving them their outbursts and irresponsible behavior. We must realize that there is a much larger principle at stake here and attempt to provide an environment in which our grandchildren can grow into normalcy and somehow escape the ravages that divorce breeds.[4]

Money Matters

Unfortunately, another major element can complicate things, and may also prolong the period of adjustment to a divorce. It's called money.

Your son may need or want to borrow from you to pay the rent during a separation.

You may be approaching retirement, and find yourself pulled between saving for yourself and helping your son with the bills after he was awarded custody of the three children.

You may be upset over your son's irresponsible behavior financially, and decide to assist your daughter-in-law and the children rather than him.

You may be struggling about having given your ex-daughter-in-law some family heirlooms, never dreaming that there would be a divorce and that she would keep the heirlooms.

You gave the couple the down payment on their new home as a wedding gift, but now the home is hers.

Some financial issues may pertain to past gifts and loans. But you can do little about those. You can plan for the future. Parents of a divorced child have asked questions such as:

How can I be sure my son's ex doesn't receive any of his inheritance?

How can I be sure my ex-daughter-in-law doesn't misuse funds I've set aside for the grandchildren?

How can I get out of business arrangements with my ex-daughter-in-law and her family?

Just as your son needs assistance from an attorney, you may find yourself in the same situation.

New Branches on the Family Tree

In time, a semblance of stability may be reached, only to be upset again when you learn that your family tree is about to have some unfamiliar branches grafted onto it. Your son has just told you that he is getting married again...to a woman with three children. You are going to be an instant step-grandparent. It is out of your control, and you have no choice in the matter.

Sometimes, however, you can't help but resist. Several common problems can occur—all of which need to be avoided.

The new spouse is not welcomed in her new in-laws' home, or at best she is politely tolerated. I have seen situations in which the new marriage was not even recognized. The new wife was referred to as "that woman and her children." This is classic, unhealthy denial! In some cases the new marriage is sabotaged by the grandparents through rejection, manipulation or spreading rumors.

Sometimes the new spouse is accepted, but the step-grandparents can't bring themselves to become involved with the new step-grandchildren. If the children are adolescents or older, this isn't so much of a problem as when they are younger.

One of the most common problems is unequal and unfair treatment of grandchildren and step-grandchildren. This is a difficult situation because the grandparents' feelings for their original grandchildren are usually positive, and it is natural for them to feel that the others have been thrust upon them.

This is an issue to be discussed with the adult son and his new wife, clarifying expectations and intentions. You will have to work out some creative solutions and will find no perfect answer. Younger children have difficulty understanding preferential treatment. Older ones can learn to understand that grandparents will do more for their own grandchildren they have known from birth than for others. They can accept this as long as the differences don't blatantly emphasize feelings of being discounted and rejected.

You may want to talk with the new daughter-in-law, asking how she would like you to relate to her children and sharing your own concerns and struggles. Many who have taken this step have found some workable solutions. One step-grandmother was surprised and relieved to discover that her new daughter-in-law didn't expect her to take her children to the lake each summer as she did her own grand-children, and didn't want her to feel obligated to do so.

Feelings cannot be forced to develop. The new children may never have had the opportunity to have grandparents and you could end up filling some unmet needs. Neither side should force them-selves upon one another. Give it time. Learn how to pray specifically for the newcomers. In some cases, the new members of the family may not have been involved in church, or they may not be Chris-tians, and they can become your mission field.

Yet another problem can arise when a grandchild is born to this new marriage. The grandparents may tend to favor the new child because it is part of their family line. This will be obvious to the other step-children.

The Girl from "That Foreign Country"

Cynthia, a dignified, well-dressed woman in her early 50s, sobbed as she related to me the story of her son's wedding. Following his grad-uation from seminary, Jim felt called to the mission field. Within a year he was serving in Korea.

After a few months, he began talking about a girl he had met who worked at the same mission location. Cynthia said she thought nothing of it, and just assumed she was another missionary from the United States. But a few months later when Jim called to tell his moth-er he was getting married, she discovered that his bride-to-be was from that "foreign country," as she called it. And the wedding would be held in Korea in just six weeks.

"It was such a shock, especially when we arrived there," Cynthia said. "Everything was so different, from the food to all the customs. And her family didn't speak English. We had to use a translator, and it was so hard. I felt so out of place, so lost and so disappointed.

"And the wedding service was not like it was here at all! Jim's wife doesn't speak English that well, so we really don't communicate much. I just don't know what's going to happen in the future. It looks like Jim is learning to fit into that culture, and we're being left out."

Everyone who gets married marries a foreigner to one degree or another, but a child marrying someone of another race is not something most parents expect.

Another family I know wrote about their experiences when both their son and daughter married a person from another race. This was part of their reaction to their son Mark's announcement of whom he was dating:

> As far as we can remember, we never discussed the subject of interracial marriage with our children. It was a nonissue. We assumed that they would eventually marry individuals of their own race. Fred's mother had often commented that "birds of a feather flock together." It was understood that casual friendships with people who were different were fine, but dating friendships and intimate relationships should be with "our kind of people."[5]

Everyone who gets married marries a foreigner to one degree or another, but a child marrying someone of another race is not something most parents expect. Yet, cross-cultural marriages are occurring more and more, and if present trends continue they will become more commonplace. What are some ways you can prepare for it or deal with it if it has already occurred?

Motivations for Cross-Cultural Marriage

Perhaps you will be in a position to help your adult child be sure his decision to marry someone of another race is based on sound motivation. Following are some inadequate motivations that have been observed.

Some people seem to cross racial boundaries to marry because they feel like virtual *outcasts* in their own situation. Color, lack of education, or the inability to relate socially are some of the reasons for a person's perceiving himself or herself as an outcast.

Rebels exist in any culture, and some rebels marry a person of another race as a subconscious protest against their own culture. A 20-year-old who decides to protest in this way may not have the same need to protest 10 years later. But the decision of his protest is still with him.

Another kind of person who may choose a person from another culture is the *maverick*, or the nonconformist. Nonconformists usually don't care what others think, and are committed to "doing their own thing regardless of other people's response." They need to ask themselves whether such a serious step as marriage is an appropriate way to demonstrate their noncomformity.

Compensators are people who feel incomplete. They may be propelled toward marrying someone they think can fill a need in their lives. Although many compensators choose someone from their own culture, others say in effect, "If my culture can't provide me with what I need, then this other one can."

Adventurers may marry cross-culturally, especially if they identify same-race marriages as a part of the mundane world with which they are bored. The differences they encounter in a cross-cultural marriage are simply challenges that add an intensity to life.

Escapists tend to marry cross-culturally, too. They marry to improve the quality of their life, or to get away from life in their own country. I have seen this occur with foreign students attending college here in the United States. Many "war brides" do this during wartime. People may also marry a wealthy person to escape a relatively impoverished life.

Despite these inadequate motivations, it is important to realize that many interracial couples may have solid and healthy reasons for choosing one another. I've had the opportunity of working with a number of them in premarital as well as marital counseling.

Areas of Adjustment

Interracial couples face several areas in which they may be called on to make adjustments, especially if there are marked differences in culture and/or color. It takes more dedication, commitment and effort for an interracial marriage to work.

Communication: In the beginning of a cross-cultural relationship, differences in language can be intriguing; but without special care they can become a problem later. Messages can be distorted or not fully understood. A positive word in one language may be offensive in another. The humor of one culture is not necessarily the humor of another culture.

Language can affect the balance of power in a relationship. Usually, the person speaking his own language in his own country has the advantage and power. The more fluent person has more influence. Not only does the couple have to be aware of these subtleties, so do the in-laws.

But communication involves much more than language. Gestures and body language can have different meanings. Silence means different things in different cultures. The intensity of direct eye contact, and even how far you stand from the other person while speaking, often vary.

Values are very important because they tend to infuse many of the other issues involved in an interracial marriage. A value reflects what is important to the person and what may be seen as good or bad, right or wrong, important or unimportant. Values can be reflected in dress, religion, food, the way one behaves in public or when guests are entertained and morals.

Food is an issue for many. Not only the type of food or the way it is cooked and eaten, but many other factors emerge as well. One mother shared that she could hardly eat any of the food during her first visit to her married son's home, but now she has learned to enjoy it. What she doesn't like, she's learned to say no to.

Sex is an issue. Such things as contraception, menstruation, family honor, showing affection in public, personal hygiene, dancing and dress—all can be critical issues.

Male-female roles may call for adjustment. Much of this will have to do with the issue of male superiority, which differs from culture to culture. In some societies male dominance is subtle; in others it is blatant. In some cultures male-female roles blend; others have prescribed separate standards.

The *use of time* is yet another concern. What is late in one culture is not late in another. Some cultures are more relaxed and unhurried than our American system. Some people are used to eating a large meal at noon and then taking a nap. If a son marries and moves to his spouse's country, he not only has to adjust to the person but to the timetable of the country as well.

The other main adjustment areas are where the couple live, politics, friends, finances, in-laws, social class, religion, dealing with stress, illness and suffering and raising children.

Inadequate Parental Responses

Some parents react negatively to an adult child's decision to marry someone from another culture. One response is denial. It can be as extreme as not having pictures of the couple in the house, or refusing to accept or discuss the marriage.

Another common response is being apologetic. Parents who are embarrassed by their adult son's or daughter's decision to marry across racial lines may apologize every time they mention it to someone. The purpose is often to obtain sympathy and support for your concern. Often the marriage is seen as a tragedy and thus can dominate the conversation.

Other parents accept their adult child's decision, but don't necessarily approve of it. They say, "It's his life and his decision. We wish he hadn't made this choice, but we'll learn to live with it."

A More Positive Way

Some parents are supportive, and make an effort to accept the marriage partner their adult child has chosen. They are willing to learn about the culture of their new son- or daughter-in-law. They take a more positive approach toward telling others.

Fred and Anita Prinzing, the couple referred to earlier, made this effort and found it to be rewarding. As they opened themselves to their daughter-in-law Martha, they progressed from shyness and hesitance to more open communication. Eventually they were able to have conversations like this:

> During a recent visit, Martha asked Anita something she'd wanted to know for a long time. "Mom, were you more concerned with my background or my skin color when Mark and I wanted to be married?"
>
> Anita knew she had to be truthful. Selecting her words with care, she answered, "Martha, I'm ashamed to admit this, but it was only your skin color that bothered me."
>
> Martha was surprised. "I always thought it was my background," she said.
>
> Their discussion could never have taken place during the first few years of their acquaintance, as Martha almost never initiated a conversation. Frightened and shy of her northern, educated in-laws, she politely answered our questions with one or two words. Today Martha is a college student and a wife and mother of two active children. Her newfound confidence has given her courage to ask questions that have bothered her for many years.[6]

The Prinzings cite the apostle Paul's statement, "From now on we regard no one from a worldly point of view" (2 Cor. 5:16, *NIV*). They affirm that interracial marriages can provide the opportunity to see people from God's viewpoint, not to judge them by the color of their skin but by the clarity of our vision.

Lifestyles and Tough Love

Today we are facing a new generation who has a different set of values and morals. Parents are shocked and frustrated over their adolescent son's choice of dress, friends, lifestyle, sexual preference, attitudes, education (or lack of) and vocation. Following are three specific areas in which such frustrations are often experienced.

Drugs and Other Dependencies

I have seen the use of alcohol and drugs cause a marriage to self-destruct. One mother told me, "It's such a shock. Jim never drank or used drugs as a teen nor through college. And now to discover he's been using up his and his wife's income to support his cocaine habit is just too much. And to think we lent him several thousand dollars last year to get his business going! It all went for drug use."

When parents have invested years and tears in an adult son, only to see him destroy his life with drug abuse, it is natural for them not only to be shocked but to try to help. The difficulty is that parents are sometimes the last persons an adult child will listen to.

At the other extreme, some adult children expect criticism—perhaps even preaching!—from their parents, and in some strange way actually depend on this reproach to justify their habit. This can easily lead to a "codependent" relationship, and you as a parent providing the very means of your son's dependency.

The goal of parents, whose son's lifestyle they reject, should be to make their value system clear, and to show loving concern, without being lured into the codependency trap. They will need to practice "detachment." This does not mean aloofness or disdain or rejection. It means that they free themselves from compulsions to correct their son's behavior for him. It means that they communicate by their actions that they have their own lives to live, and that their adult child is responsible for his life.

Melody Beattie writes of the positive results of such detachment, and how it can be much more helpful to an adult child living an addictive lifestyle than any amount of scolding or preaching:

> Sometimes detachment even motivates and frees people around us to begin to solve their problems. We stop worrying about them, and they pick up the slack and finally start worrying about themselves. What a grand plan! We each mind our own business.[7]

Extramarital Relationships

It can be heartrending for the parents of an adult child to learn that their own son has been unfaithful to his wife, or that he has otherwise sought sexual relationships beyond the boundaries clearly set by the Scriptures.

How do you handle it if you are told by your son that he is homosexual, and that his involvement with his "boyfriends" has destroyed his marriage? What explanation do you give your three grandchildren when they ask why their parents are breaking up? Or perhaps the divorce is stemming from your daughter-in-law's revelation that she is a lesbian. And how would you deal with your concerns about the possibility of AIDS and other sexually transmitted diseases?

In such situations, parents of adult children often ask themselves several questions: What was our contribution to this problem? Where did we go wrong? Why didn't we see any indications of homosexuality when he was young? Did we just close our eyes to them? How do we explain the reason for the breakup to our friends? Some basic considerations can bring stability in an otherwise uncertain time when such events occur.

Individuation and Your Son's Values

Parents often have trouble distinguishing the personality boundaries between themselves and an adult son when he rejects the values he was taught. They may feel that something in their parenting was an unwitting invitation to their son to somehow become involved in a lifestyle that was foreign to what the parents openly espoused.

It may be helpful to remember that one way adult children become adult is through the process of individuation—consciously and unconsciously separating themselves from their parents.

Although parents may agonize over their adult child's lifestyle choices, they can only affirm this process of becoming an individual. They need not second-guess their parenting styles, or their own values and ideals regarding sexuality. Instead, they can reaffirm that they and their adult child are separate persons, able to make differing choices regardless of having come from the same family—even if you strongly disagree with his choice.

Your son's extramarital lifestyle will require you to find a balance between accepting him as a person, and as your son, while making it clear you reject his actions. Usually the parent-child relationship is so close that you won't need to make long or frequent speeches to communicate your disappointment. You may want to be honest about any anger. But the same process of individuating that led him to adopt a different set of values means he will likely resist any sermonizing or tongue-lashing you may feel like delivering.

Parents in this situation can certainly reaffirm their own value system by means such as making it clear that their son's illicit partner won't spend the night on any visits to their home. When others bring up the subject, they can certainly affirm their own feelings and values. It is never an easy situation, but a course must be sought that allows you both to affirm your son as having been made in the image of God, while standing firmly for God's will for His creatures.

Telling and Not Telling

Parents of adult children do not need to tell others more than they wish. Honesty can prevail, while being discreet, and describing their son's situation in general rather than specific terms. Although saying something such as, "They just reached a point where their marriage couldn't work" may not satisfy some people, true friends will respect your right to privacy, and that of your son.

Such discreetness can be balanced by confiding with a pastor, counselor or an especially close friend, and sharing the truth with them in order not to lapse into denial or unwisely block your feelings.

But remember that your son may work through this problem and return to a biblical lifestyle. If he does, you will regret having broadcast the news of his problem, especially if you did it out of anger and retaliation.

When Your Faith Is Rejected

Sylvia Vogel, a Jewish mother, faced a different kind of disappointment in her relationship with her adult daughter Ellen:

> From the beginning, the mother was aware of the implications of her daughter's actions. Yet she was unable to stop them. On Mother's Day, [she] received word that the Moonies had picked her Jewish daughter and a black seminary student she hardly knew as one of 705 "perfect matches" for marriage.[8]

Even if the break from the parents' faith is not as drastic as this, any deviation from so precious a heritage as a family's traditional belief in God can be traumatic. Again, some parents suffer from guilt when this happens. Doesn't the Bible say that if you bring up your child in the way he should go, when he is old he won't depart from it? (See Proverbs 22:6.)

The fact is, you may not have been perfect in training your child in a religious faith. But accepting imperfection, as we have previously noted, is often the first step toward healing a wound. One father shared with his pastor his feelings of guilt over a grown daughter who had rejected his faith. "I was busy having a midlife crisis about the time my daughter was a teenager, and struggling with her faith," said the father. "And my wife and I were struggling in our marriage. I don't think I did a very good job of handing along my faith at a crucial time in my daughter's life."

The same free will with which we long for our children to embrace our faith can lead them to embrace another faith—or none.

Although he was genuinely upset, the man half expected his pastor's response to consist of some "There-there salve" to deny that the man had been an inadequate parent, and to give some soothing words of reassurance. Instead, his wise pastor said, "Well, you're probably right, to some extent. Your daughter needed an example of faith as a teen. *But you know that His grace can cover both your failure and your daughter.*"

Also, what has been said about individuation is certainly a factor in an adult child's faith development. Few parents really wish their children were robots who automatically responded to the way they were programmed. The same free will with which we long for our children to embrace our faith can lead them to embrace another faith—or none. At times this may seem to be an imperfect arrangement, but it is the way God made us. And the prophet Isaiah asks:

> "Does the clay say to the potter, 'What are you making?'...This is what the Lord says—the Holy One of Israel, and its Maker:...do you question me about my children, or give me orders about the work of my hands?" (Isa. 45:9,11, *NIV*).

Some parents in this situation have found that at least they are allowed to take the grandchildren to church with them. Whether this is possible or not, it is important to remember the principle the apostle Peter laid down regarding believing wives' behavior toward their unbelieving husbands. They should *live* their faith instead of *preaching* it to their husbands, "so that, if any of them do not believe the word, they may be won over without words by the behavior of their wives" (1 Pet. 3:1, *NIV*).

These are just some of the adjustments that are part of the surprise package some parents of adult children receive. Events such as these can bring both losses and gains. They are times when your faith and God's strength will be your stability.

Reflecting on This Chapter

1. Did (or do) any of your young children seem to specialize in doing the daring or the unexpected? How did (do) you respond to their escapades?

2. Have you or any other parents you know experienced the divorce of a son or daughter? What was your (their) reaction? Could it have been handled better?

3. Have you or any other parents you know been faced with adjusting to a son's or daughter's remarriage? Could it have been handled better?

4. Have any disappointments or unexpected turns of events with your adult child caused tension between you and your spouse? How was it handled?

5. Have any such disappointments caused you to blame yourself or others? If you haven't moved beyond the blaming stage, what more positive response can you make?

6. If you are a grandparent, have you helped deal with any insecurities among your grandchildren? How?

7. Has your empty nest ever been filled again? What adjustments were required?

8. How have you or any other parents you know dealt with an interracial marriage?

9. Have you had a problem accepting an adult child's lifestyle? If so, how have you handled it?

10. How have you or other parents you know dealt with an adult child who has not adopted his or her parents' faith?

Recommended Reading:

Joyce and Norm Wright, *I'll Love You Forever* (Colorado Springs, CO: Focus on the Family, 1993).

Notes

1. Dorothy Weiss Gottlieb, Inez Bellow Gottlieb and Marjorie A. Slavin,

What to Do When Your Son or Daughter Divorces (New York: Bantam Books, 1988), p. 37.

2. Ibid., pp. 119-120.
3. Jay Kesler, *Grandparenting: The Agony and the Ecstasy* (Ann Arbor, MI: Servant Publications, 1993), p. 16.
4. Ibid.
5. Fred and Anita Prinzing, *Mixed Messages* (Chicago, IL: Moody Press, 1991), pp. 16-17.
6. Ibid., pp. 149-150.
7. Melody Beattie, *Codependent No More* (San Francisco, CA: HarperSanFrancisco, 1987), p. 57.
8. Joy P. Gage, *When Parents Cry* (Denver, CO: Accent Books, 1980), pp. 16-17.

𝒜 Tribute
to
My Own Mother

I WOULD LIKE TO TELL YOU ABOUT ONE MOTHER—MY OWN.

Her name was Amelia Nette Theresa Cornelius. My mother was born in 1900 and was the third of eight children. She started out in the horse-and-buggy days and lived to hear about the Space Probe to Mars, as well as men walking on the moon

She survived the rigors of growing up on a farm, including running a pitchfork through her foot and sustaining back injuries when her horse raced through a low door in the barn. She learned to work hard, plowing and harvesting the fields. She held a light for her father as he constructed one of the first homemade tractors. During the winter, she either walked several miles through the snow to school or skated to school on the frozen Sioux River. She plowed corn, experienced raging blizzards and had encounters with gypsies who camped on their farm.

Although living on the farm, she rubbed elbows with those who later became famous. Her classmate at the Canton, South Dakota, high school was Ernest Lawrence, who invented the atom-smashing cyclotron. Later she worked in a Huron, South Dakota, drugstore where the owner's young son, Hubert H. Humphrey, played in the aisles of the store.

Mom married for the first time at age 19. As an airplane mechanic in World War I, her husband flew with pilots to test the plane, but on two occasions crashed and sustained hidden injuries. After they married, they began an odyssey of moves, which would eventually bring them to California. They drove an old car in which they also slept; they cooked their food in a pan on two stones over a fire. When the car broke down, her husband took it apart and repaired it himself, as there were no tow trucks or repair shops. They often bogged down in the foot-deep sand that made up many of the roads.

When their car finally died in Barstow, California, they abandoned it 200 miles from Los Angeles, hitched a ride, and stayed with a couple who had given them transportation to this emerging city. In time, they searched out the hills above Hollywood and discovered a beautiful canyon with abundant brush, trees and wildlife. Here they began to settle like pioneers on the prairie. The down payment on the lot was 10 dollars!

They rented a one-room shack in the hills while they built their first home. Constructed without benefit of a level, this house is still livable today. Without sewers, a cesspool had to suffice. In 1925, they were able to move into another house. Mom's farming background was not forgotten as she planted fruit trees, vegetables and all kinds of flowers. Now and then they would attend a new church in Los Angeles called Angeles Temple. It was founded by a young woman minister by the name of Aimee Semple McPherson.

Both my mom and her husband, Paul, worked hard on the homes, in addition to holding down full-time jobs. As a manager for a bakery, the way Mom handled some of her responsibilities reflected her strength and independence. One day a man came in, ripped the phone off the hook, and demanded the keys to the safe. But she slipped out the back and called the police, who quickly apprehended him. When someone followed her one dark night as she walked the three miles to her home in the hills, Mother outran him. She also had to be assertive when a movie personality by the name of Hopalong Cassidy asked her out on a date. She quickly let him know that she was married.

Her first son Paul was born in 1930. Four years later tragedy struck when her husband suddenly died of a stroke.

In 1937, Mom married my dad, a widower who was 12 years older than her. I was born when Mom was 37 years of age and Dad was 49. She worked hard raising both my half-brother and me, as well as taking care of three other rental houses.

Our family encouraged the enjoyment of life as well as the values of honesty, hard work and getting a thorough education. My parents sacrificed to give us experiences and opportunities that had not been available to them. We went on trips and were given music lessons. As a family, we saw practically every movie produced in Hollywood during the '40s. If Dad was busy working, Mom filled in playing baseball, taking me fishing as well as hunting.

Living in the Hollywood canyon area was similar to growing up in the country, having the added resources of a large metropolitan city just minutes away. My brother and I developed an appreciation for animals and the outdoors, while avoiding some of the pressures of city life. Mom taught us how to help repair the rental homes, including painting, tar papering roofs, laying linoleum and cleaning out sewer pipes.

She survived floods, fires and earthquakes while living in Laurel Canyon. Here was a women whose values reflected her early years as well as her family's background. Wanting us to develop our potential to the fullest, she encouraged us, helped us in any way possible when we struggled, corrected us when necessary and demonstrated compassion. She spoke her mind and was definite, but she listened and considered others' opinions and beliefs. Mom passed on a strong legacy, a rich heritage from her side of the family. As a result, my brother and I have a better sense of who we are individually and as a family.

Mom was widowed a second time in 1960 when my dad was killed in an auto accident at the age of 72. She did not slow down though; she used her time baby-sitting for families in Laurel Canyon and Beverly Hills. She also took art lessons and started painting scenic and still life pictures, amazing even herself with the latent talent. While her health permitted, she traveled; she visited England, France, Germany, Switzerland, Russia, Italy, the Holy Land, Hawaii, Alaska, the world's fair in Seattle and more. She was an active participant, not just another sightseer; smuggling Bibles into Moscow, riding in a kayak and dancing with an Alaskan sourdough in Nome, going to the top of the Eiffel Tower in Paris and a bell tower in Switzerland. She would have taken a ride in an ultralight aircraft at a Montana airport at age 80, and was disappointed when there was not enough room for her!

Finally, in her late 70s, Mom sold her houses and moved into a retirement center near me. Even into her 90s she continued to raise the flowers she had always loved.

At the age of 90, she concluded her own written life history with this poignant description of the retirement center: "When I first moved here, I attended all the activities such as trips and concerts and had so many friends. By 1989, I lost virtually all my friends to death and now, along with crippling arthritis, I feel very lonely here Where I'll go from here only God knows."

In her last illness, the doctor said, "In 93 years, a lot of the parts just wear out." But two things never wore out: her spirit, and her love of family—her kids, grandkids, great-grandchildren, and nephews and nieces of at least three generations.

In recent conversations, she said she realized it was just a matter of time; she was just waiting for the Lord to call her. For several months her health deteriorated, including another bout with cancer and then a stroke. It was during these months that this book was being written.

On Wednesday, October 13, 1993, she received her final assignment. Her work here was complete after 93 years.

Now there is a new resident in heaven where she has no more

pain or tears. In the home-going services for Mom, whom I miss, I recall the statement, "When you say good-bye to a loved one who is a believer, remember at that moment they are saying hello to Jesus Christ." My mom is there along with my son, Matthew.

I am so thankful for the mother who influenced and loved me—Amelia Nette Theresa Wright.

Discussion Leader's Guide

THIS BOOK CAN BE USED AS A LIVELY AND HELPFUL RESOURCE FOR A STUDY OR discussion group. The following guidelines will help you organize and conduct a series that will benefit various family members, especially wives. But don't automatically assume husbands and mothers-in-law won't enjoy it, too!

The optimum-sized discussion group is 10 to 15 people. A smaller group may tail off in interest unless there is an unusually high level of commitment to participate regularly. A larger group will require strong leadership skills to help everyone participate meaningfully.

If you are leading a group that already meets regularly, such as a Sunday School class, decide how many weeks to spend on the series. Be sure to plan for any holidays that may come during the time you schedule the group's meetings.

Using a little creativity, the nine chapters of this book can be made to fit a regular 13-week quarter. For example, you may want to choose four of the chapters to divide into two sessions. Or consider inviting a guest speaker for one or more of the sessions. Yet another approach is to "spin off" a topic such as second marriages or lifestyles and in-law relationships for a session of its own, drawing your discussion material from the experiences of class members.

Also, you may want to have a separate introductory session along the following lines. Either in small groups (up to six or seven people) or the entire group together, lead class members in a time of getting better acquainted. The discussion can be spontaneous and informal, or you can suggest questions that, although nonthreatening, still help the class members get to know each other better:

1. On a scale of 1 to 10, 10 being "couldn't be better," how would you rate your in-law relationships? Why?
2. Describe an ideal mother-in-law.
3. In what ways is your husband like his mother?
4. What are some common mother-in-law stereotypes, and what do you think of them?
5. If you could give your own son one gift that would help him have good in-law relationships, what would it be?
6. What is the best (or worst) parental advice you ever received?

Such questions can help class members identify with each other, and discover what they have in common.

Don't overlook the way the class members' own questions can contribute to the relevance of the study to their own lives. If dealing with such questions as they arise makes it difficult to cover the material in a given chapter, encourage class members to write them down. Perhaps they can be grouped together and dealt with in a special session. If you have a guest speaker such as a counselor or minister, perhaps they can deal with the issues class members have raised.

You, or someone you appoint, could act as group organizer, inviting others and perhaps calling class members to remind them of meeting dates, times and places.

Think about details such as whether refreshments will be served, and whether child care should be arranged. In most cases, people will put more into the group if they are responsible for buying their own copy of the book.

You will probably not have to provide Bibles, because the Scriptures referred to in this book are printed in the text. This feature will help people who have little or no background of the Bible, eliminating the need to find specific references.

Be aware of basic principles of group dynamics, such as:

1. Arrange seating in a semicircle, the leader included instead of standing in front. This allows the setting to invite participation.
2. The following tips are helpful in guiding discussions:

   a. Accept statements from group members without judgmentalism, even if you disagree with them. If they are clearly unbiblical or unfair, you can ask questions that clarify the issue; but outright rejection of comments is a good way to stifle open participation.

   b. If a question or comment is off the subject, either suggest that it be dealt with at another time or ask the group if they would prefer to pursue the new issue now.

   c. If someone talks too much, direct a few questions specifically to someone else. Or, tactfully interrupt the dominator by saying something like, "Excuse me, that's a good thought, and I wonder what some of the rest of us think about that." Sometimes you can talk with the person privately and enlist his or her help in drawing others into the discussion.

   d. Make it easy and comfortable for everyone to share or ask questions, but don't force anyone to do so. Sometimes reluctant participants can warm to the idea of sharing by being asked to read a passage from the book. You can also pair a shy person with someone else for a discussion apart from the main group, and ask reluctant participants to write down a conclusion to be shared with the larger group.

e. If someone asks you a question and you don't know the answer, admit it and move on. If the question calls for insight from personal experience, invite others to comment on it. If it requires special knowledge, offer to look for an answer in the library or from a counselor or minister, and report later on your findings.

3. Unless the group leader is a therapist or other professional trained in counseling, guard against trying to do group therapy. This doesn't mean that poignant moments won't come up or unhappy problems won't be shared, but the group is for sharing, not treating or fixing. The leader should be open and honest about wanting to grow with the group instead of coming across as an authoritative master of in-law relationships.

4. Start and stop on time, according to the schedule agreed on before the series begins, for the benefit of people's own schedules.

5. In each session, lead group members in discussing the questions and exercises at the end of each chapter, unless you sense that some of them might be too sensitive to be appropriately discussed in a group such as this. If you have more than 8 or 10 class members, consider assigning some of the questions to be discussed in smaller groups, then invite each group to share one or two insights with the larger group.

6. Pray regularly for the sessions and the participants. God will honor your willingness to guide people toward more fruitful relationships.